The Fall and Redemption of Man
and
The Will of God

The Fall and Redemption of Man and The Will of God

Dr. Paul A. Dewhirst

PENTLAND PRESS, INC.
ENGLAND • USA • SCOTLAND

PUBLISHED BY PENTLAND PRESS, INC.
5124 Bur Oak Circle, Raleigh, North Carolina 27612
United States of America
919-782-0281

ISBN 1-57197-046-0
Library of Congress Catalog Card Number 96-71762

Copyright © 1997 Dr. Paul A. Dewhirst

All rights reserved, which includes the right to reproduce this book or portions thereof in any form whatsoever except as provided by the U.S. Copyright Law.

Printed in the United States of America

Dedicated to Vivian Opal Harrison, who has given of her time relentlessly for the last four years in feeding my handwritten thoughts into her computer, making changes as I would rewrite sentences, paragraphs, and even pages. We had a common objective: to share the message it carried with others to God's glory and unto the fulfillment of man's created potential.

My dear wife of sixty-nine years and I, with mutual endearment for Opal, are single in our thoughts that she is the one worthy of this honor.

Contents

Foreword	viii
The Fall and Redemption of Man	1
The Fall and Redemption of Man - Part I	3
The Fall and Redemption of Man - Part II	18
The Fall and Redemption of Man - Part III	26
The Fall and Redemption of Man - Part IV	42
The Fall and Redemption of Man - Part V	59
Summary	75
A Review	77
The Will of God	89
The Will of God - Part I	91
God's Standard of Righteousness - Part II	99
God's Administrative Order of Righteousness - Part III	110
God's Recompensing Judgments - Part IV	122
Appendix A	131
Appendix B	134
Appendix C	136
Appendix D	142

Foreword

I have had several, who have read my manuscript, ask how I came into the knowledge of the message I am sharing in this book. As far as I know it is a further unveiling of truth not addressed before. The revelation God is giving of Himself is a progressive unveiling of the truth. Whatever one holds for the truth must be answerable to challenge.

One who declares one's personal convictions is making room for a further unveiling of the truth of God in one's own heart and in the hearts of others. When God is given the preeminence, the Holy Spirit will ungarble the message to make a blessing which is of God.

I had had fifteen years of Bible conference ministry prior to 1960-1961, when I was teamed with Dr. Roddy, Professor of Homiletics, Fuller Theological Seminary, for a week of ministry at Forest Home. I had the morning service each day. The subject I addressed was "The Sanctity of the Home." Dr. Roddy had the evening service—subjectively evangelistic. We were speaking to a select group, college aged delegates representing the leadership of some fifteen churches—possibly numbering 150 or more youth in the prime of their lives.

Their concepts of salvation were too legal to have been spiritually or personally effective in their lives. Their faith was built on the vicarious theory of the atonement. From what I learned at this conference, I saw that it was too licensing and too self-serving to be the whole truth. I felt too keenly the responsibility and accountability of my stewardship to God not to heed revelation that was obviously of Him.

I decided then that I would not take another Bible conference until I had given further thought and study on the subjects of the atonement and redemption. We either did not have the truth, or if we did, it was not being communicated.

I left the conference for home deeply disturbed in spirit. I shared the burden of my heart with my wife. No one was any closer to my heart or could have been more understanding of what we faced together—what to do. Many weeks of the year, Elba was home alone with our German shepherd dog, Sally, but in spirit with me in my Bible conference ministry. Never did I hear a complaint from her. Her life was wholly given to being a wife and a mother to God's glory. What a gem! What a mate to have for life! At this writing over sixty-nine years. Bless God!!

After having given prayerful thought on what to do, we decided to sell our house in Los Angeles, buy a cabin at Big Bear Lake, and move. This worked out very well for what I had in mind. We did not know at the time this cabin would be our home for the next two years.

My objective was given priority on my time. I had gleaned knowledge from the writings of many men of God of different schools of theology. I was well informed. My mind had not been programmed by any one school, allowing me to pursue my objective with an open mind. I carefully studied the Bible on the subject of the atonement, and scrutinized more closely what I had held to be the truth. It is amazing to me the thoughts that came to my mind that had not been entertained by others before, to my knowledge.

Following our time spent at Big Bear Lake, I resumed my Bible conference ministry. My first conference was at the invitation of Pastor Leland Wilkinson, pastor of a Baptist church in Aberdeen, Washington.

En route, I met with Dr. John Houser, pastor of the First Baptist Church, Corvallis, Oregon. Dr. Houser served on the Board of Directors of Western Theological Seminary; he was a man of God, and highly revered in the Northwest. What was scheduled for one hour turned out to be three hours. His knowledge of the Scriptures made our discussion of the subject mutually profitable. He could not have been more responsive to what he was hearing: the truth will bear testimony to one's heart that it is of God. I left Corvallis blessing God.

I had the same kind of response from Pastor Leland Wilkinson in Aberdeen, Washington. It is rare to find a man so dedicated to his convictions. Hearing the message changed the course of his ministry at great personal sacrifice to him the rest of his days.

I kept no record of the Bible conferences I have had; no dates, and, most regrettably, no notes on the subjects addressed. I never used notes in speaking. God had gifted me in communicating, and in thinking on my feet. I always had my message well in mind, and the spiritual pulse of my audience; I could sense what was not being understood. I would make windows spontaneously to let in more light on the subject. It is amazing what a homey story pertinent to the message will do to sharpen interest.

I can remember some of my conferences better than others. At the age of ninety-two, I have probably forgotten more than I can remember. This I do remember, that it was the message that endeared my listeners to God. The message did not excite guilt, lend to despair, or threaten condemnation. It gave hope.

I remember speaking daily for one week at Multanomah School of the Bible. There was not one student or faculty member who did not sense the presence of God. All in attendance will remember this week of services, as I do. On campus, one student, in a respectful manner, asked me what my credentials were. I answered her, "The blessings of God on the message."

In August 1970, we moved from the southern part of the state to our retirement home in Paradise, California. We had no more become settled, when the pastor of the First Baptist Church of Paradise called on us. His visit was cordial; he showed the warmth of a kindred spirit. Before leaving, he asked to engage me for a series of meetings. He had heard of the blessings of God on the message of my ministry. I made one request of him: that I have the Sunday morning service just prior to the series of meetings. Interest was enkindled in their hearts. We had a full sanctuary attendance every Wednesday night for the whole series. The blessing of God on those meetings introduced my ministry to Paradise and the vicinity. For the next few years, my ministry was mostly limited to pulpit supply.

I had been ministering in the area for possibly five years when I received a telephone call from the chairman of the program committee of the Evangelical Free Church Pastor's Association of Northern California. He was pastor of the Sacramento Church. He asked me to be the speaker for their pastor's retreat, then being planned. We had never met, nor had he heard me speak. From what he told me, he was well informed of the blessings of God on the message of my ministry.

As I recall, the retreat was for three days. I spoke Friday evening, three times on Saturday, and once Sunday morning. All pastors were back in their respective churches for Sunday evening service, echoing the ministry of the conference.

There were possibly fifty pastors and a few of their elders with them in attendance. I could not have addressed a more attentive audience. They were hearing a message they had not heard before: the fall and redemption of man presented from a spiritual premise. I felt privileged by God to have this ministry that had the potential of reaching some fifty congregations as it was shared by their respective pastors. From the number of pastors who talked with me privately, I learned that the message was being made clear, and bore witness of the truth to their hearts.

The personal convictions in one's heart will be shared with others. This conference, which touched the hearts of so many pastors, opened many more doors of ministry for me. The message those pastors heard I am now sharing with my reader in this book. Read and be blessed of God.

THE FALL AND REDEMPTION OF MAN

Part I
The Fall and Redemption of Man

One must believe that God is the lover of our souls and the rewarder of those who diligently seek Him. God created man that He might share His life with him to God's glory and to man's fulfillment. More than anything else, God wants our hearts and the communion of our fellowship. Man is incomplete apart from being in a living bond to God. Spiritual bonds are made secure by a responsive love to God's love, by a child's love to parental love, by the love of sweethearts for each other, and the like. There is no greater magnetic power in the spiritual realm than that of love. It is not until God's love for one becomes revelation to one that it will engender a responsive love for God and create a kindred spirit with God. The most revealing manifestation of love is the Divine family, wherein all three members are essentially love.

There is no way of knowing, apart from what is written in the Bible, what took place in eternity before time whereby one can discern a continuity with which one can relate, and be given a greater insight into the heart of God. Enough of sacred history is given to carry us back into eternity wherein we can perceive the glorious relationship within the family bonds of the Holy Trinity, before the world was.

God is spirit and, no less, personality. God identified Himself to Moses by the name, I AM. The name not only infers His essential being but also His personal presence. The social quality inheres in personality. God speaks in the first person; is self-affirmative and self-communicative. In Him, there is an active commerce of thought and affection which gives support to the doctrine of the Trinity: God the

Father, God the Son, and God the Holy Spirit, three persons, one God, one Divine family in perfect unity with attributes in common.

God the Son is the only begotten Son of God, the only issue of God the Father and God the Holy Spirit. The personalities of God the Father and God the Holy Spirit are inclusive of each other; are expressive of themselves as of one person. What was in the mind of one would be congruous with what was in the mind of the other. The Son's personality is exclusive of the Father's, but is in perfect accord with the Father: a perfect Father-Son relationship. The attributes of the Son are in common with those of the Father. He is God; He is Spirit; He is holy; He is infinite, immutable, omnipotent, omnipresent, loving, merciful, righteous, and just. His Divine nature and Sonship are by eternal generation.

I refer my reader to Proverbs, chapter eight. Wisdom crieth to awaken the sons of men to an understanding of God, His love, His righteousness, and the inheritance awaiting those who love Him. It was already possessed by the Son of God in eternity, before creation. "I was set up from everlasting, from the beginning, or ever the earth was. Then I was by Him, as one brought up with Him: and I was daily His delight, rejoicing always before Him; Rejoicing in the habitable part of His earth; and my delights were with the sons of men" (Prov. 8:23,30-31). The glorious relationship between God the Father and His only begotten Son is too directly related in the context to be interpreted otherwise. It is revealing of their endearment for each other and an insight into the heart of the Divine family. Their thoughts objectively were in sharing their life and the joys of celestial glory with the sons of men—an outreach of infinite love.

"In the beginning God created the heaven and the earth" (Gen. 1:1). The Hebrew word Elohim, translated God, is plural, but the construction is uniformly singular, and governs a singular verb. Elohim identifies properly the God of creation, the Triune God, three persons, one God. What God said, "Let us make man" (Gen. 1:26), gives further support to the Triune concept of God. "Us" is inclusive of more than one. In Hebrew, the plural is often used to express the superlative, the greatest, the most. The plural usage of Elohim in the context expresses the superlative, the singleness of greatness, the only true and living God.

The Hebrew word, translated "created," is *bara* and means to bring into being something that didn't exist before. God's objective in creating the world was to make it habitable for the sons of men. The grandeur of creation makes manifest the love God has in His heart for man and the anticipation He had in sharing His life with man. Everything that was made was with man in mind.

The earth was landscaped with beautiful trees and shrubs having complementary shades of foliage and color, with flowering rose bushes and plants of all varieties: a feast for the eyes and a fragrance to the sense of smell. Edibles of all kinds were in abundance. All living creatures were subject to man's dominion and were essential in keeping the world of nature in balance: a creation with which man could be interestingly involved.

Man was the capstone of creation. All else created would have been pointless apart from him. God, being Spirit, couldn't have had any personal interest in creation apart from man. No wonder the Psalmist acclaims, "What is man that thou art mindful of him? and the son of man, that thou visitest him?" (Psalms 8:4).

With all of creation in place, God saw that it was good and said, "Let us make man in our image, after our likeness" (Gen. 1:26): a created personality with an innate proclivity Godward. All of creation was a family project: God the Father and God the Holy Spirit were functionally complementary to the only begotten Son of God in bringing it all to pass. "So God created man in his own image, in the image of God created he him; male and female created he them" (Gen. 1:27).

The man and the woman were spiritually constituted to be complete in a living bond to God and to each other, and genetically constituted to bring forth after their kind. The family bond was a part of the image of God man was created to bear and perpetuate. The home is of God's making and is the basic unit of society. One's spiritual heritage is a strong influence in one's life; like father, like son. When the spirit of love for God and for each other pervades the home, it will be a foretaste of the heavenly home of all believers—members of the family of God by adoption.

It is hard for one to conceive, apart from a contrast with which one can relate, how wonderful the thoughts of God are of the sons of men: to have created man in His own image; for it to be innate in man to have loving family bonds like the Divine family of God. When family bonds lose their values by God's standard of righteousness, and their respect of parental guidance, it will be an era of self-serving objectives. Hearts will be hardened toward God and toward each other; a spirit of anarchy will prevail. Special interest groups will be voiced; will get louder, bolder, more demanding, and finally explode in violence. When God is given the preeminence in the home, it will not be this way.

God is. There is no time factor in His essential being. God is the same yesterday, today, and forever. Man's thoughts of God are according to circumstances with which man can relate, even though they were spiritually wrought in eternity before time. God's personal interaction with man is always in the present tense. God's foreknowledge is inclusive of His omniscience and in no way affects His personal responses as He relates to man, nor does man's foreknowledge affect his personal responses or the exercise of his free agency as he relates to God and to each other. Man knows that his loved ones are going to die, but his foreknowledge of this doesn't affect the personal responses he will have at the time. They will be expressed spontaneously when it happens, and will reveal what is in one's heart. The same is true of God's personal responses, only with God there is no time factor. They are the same whether they find expression in eternity or in time. His delights with the sons of men before the world was are the same in time. God doesn't change.

God the Father said unto Jesus, "Thou art my Son, today have I begotten thee" (Heb. 5:5, Psalms 2:7). Today is not a calendar date, but the timeless state of the only begotten Son of God. His divine nature and Sonship are by eternal generation. He was as one brought up with the Father and was daily His delight, rejoicing always before Him.

The endearment of the Father to the Son and the Son to the Father finds expression in their personal interaction and makes manifest the bonds of infinite love. Their thoughts of the sons of men were before the world was. All of creation reveals the large place man has in the heart of God and carries a message that is but a token of God's love for him. As man gets the message, it excites an innate consciousness of a place in one's heart only God can fill. An interest is quickened as one hears of God. Not until the love of God becomes revelation in a personal way will there be a responsive love to God's love. It is when one senses another's love for oneself that personal bonds are in the making.

The love that finds expression in favorable circumstances may not reveal as much of one's love for another as that which surfaces in crucial circumstances. It is a test of how much one is willing to give of oneself to help. The spontaneity of the action taken indicates how much one's heart is in it.

The day Adam and Eve sinned, they died to the life God was sharing with them. They were lost to a living bond to God and were subjects of His mercy. The despair of man and the compassion of God met for the first time. The personal responses of God the Father and the only begotten

Son of God were spontaneous. The Father and the Son are two personalities, but are in perfect accord in the sacrificing of themselves to redeem fallen man. All sacrifices motivated by love find expression in the giving of oneself for the sake of another. No thought whatever crosses one's mind of the consequences to one's person.

It is enlightening for one to learn of the personal sacrifices the Father and Son made in the giving of themselves to redeem fallen man. What is revealed makes love a living and compelling force in one's heart. What one will do for another when motivated by love is almost unbelievable. What is true in the heart of man, created in the image of God, is true in the heart of God.

The Father gave His only begotten Son, His only issue, the One most endeared to His heart, never to have Him back again on the Divine level. The Son in full accord with the Father gave of Himself to assume manhood, self-limiting Himself to the confines of human nature. He divested Himself of His ineffable glory and the splendor of His essential being, concealing His Divine nature: a condescension inconceivable to the finite mind. The sacrifices of the Father and of the Son make manifest the depth of infinite love the finite mind cannot fathom.

In assuming human nature, the only begotten Son of God made Himself subject to God, as all of human kind. "Jesus saith unto her, 'Touch me not; for I am not yet ascended to my Father: but go to my brethren, and say unto them, I ascend unto my Father, and your Father; and to my God, and your God'" (John 20:17). He, who is equal in Divine status with God the Father, self-limited Himself to the status of human nature. This new relationship between God the Father and His only begotten Son is consequential to the giving of themselves to redeem man. Their action stemmed spontaneously from their hearts, reacting to the lapse of Adam and Eve. Their omniscience in no way affected their personal responses. The Son's relationship with the Father in eternity, after He had given of Himself to redeem man, was in His spiritual manhood. It was before He assumed His mortal manhood in time, before His spiritual manhood was incarnate. The warmth of the Father's love and the delights of celestial glory were surety to the Son, and a foretaste of the glorified manhood that would be eternally His when He had finished His mission in the mortal manhood He would assume (John 17:4-5).

God the Father appointed His only begotten Son to be the Great High Priest over all of manhood forever. The office of High Priest is an honor bestowed only on him who is called of God, as was Aaron. The Son assumed His office while in His spiritual manhood in eternity. He officiated the first rite of worship by offering Himself to His Father and His God on behalf of and in identity with fallen man, a propitiation, an acceptable offering, an atonement for the sins of the whole world. God the Father is reconciled to man. All sins shall be forgiven unto the sons of men, save the sin of unbelief. The only begotten Son of God is the High Priest, the One making the offering and the Sacrifice offered. All worship ordained by God is patterned after that of the first rite of worship offered by the Son of God in His spiritual manhood. He is the Lamb of God slain from the foundation of the world.

The name, Lamb of God, is singular to the only begotten Son of God. "The Lamb slain from the foundation of the world" has no termination, and is spiritual in character; it is inclusive of His whole humiliation: His spiritual manhood before time, His mortal manhood in time, and His glorified manhood in eternity. In identity with Him, man has a ready access to the Father. The offering of oneself, a living sacrifice, motivated by love for God, and in identity with the Lamb of God, makes one acceptable to God. All rites of worship ordained by God prefigured in type that which would be fulfilled in the person of Jesus Christ, the only begotten Son of God. It is so great to have an insight of

God's love for man that is made manifest before the world was.

"And God saw everything that he had made, and behold, it was very good. And the evening and the morning were the sixth day" (Gen. 1:31). "Thus the heavens and the earth were finished, and all the host of them. And on the seventh day God ended his work which he had made; and he rested on the seventh day from all his work which he had made" (Gen. 2:2-3).

A day in eternity cannot be reckoned in terms of time, only in a relative sense: one day in seven. The seventh day was a particular day to God. He had labored six days in providing for man, and on the seventh day entered into His rest to be with man, and as revealed, be the example for man to follow. There is no rest in the heart of man apart from his rest in God.

God, in ceasing from His works on the seventh day, also exemplified the spirit in which it was to be observed: it was to be blessed and sanctified holy unto God. We learn from the Old Covenant of the awesome holiness in which the day was hallowed; an example of the spirit in which the Lord's Day is to be observed today.

The first thoughts of God after creation were in having communion with the sons of men, with the objective of establishing the human family of God, like the Divine family of God. God wants a responsive love from man that finds expression in the spirit of worship: the Father seeks such to worship Him. It is like the man or the woman (in the spirit of devotion) seeking the love of one for the other with objective thoughts of a family bond. Communion with God in the spirit of worship is as essential to a living bond to God as communion in the spirit of devotion is to a bonding of husband and wife.

Man's only concourse to God is in the spirit of worship. God instituted worship and the home. Both are spiritual or living entities, and are interrelated. The Institution of the

Home is the embodiment of the family, while the Institution of Worship is the embodiment of collective families, a local expression of the family of God, better known as the Church. The Home is the basic unit of the Church. Man was constituted to be functionally integrated into both. He is as incomplete apart from being a member of God's family, as he is apart from being a member of his own family.

One feels at home with those of a kindred spirit in their worship of God. Their hearts are spiritually enriched as the Spirit of God ministers to them and through them to each other. The family bond is deeply rooted in the heart of God and is made manifest in the Divine family. The Institution of Worship and the Institution of the Home were intended to bear the image of the Divine family, each to be pervaded by the spirit of God and each to enjoy functional harmony to God's glory.

When the Holy Trinity is thought of in terms of family bonds, it makes for a relationship to God to which man can relate. The human family is patterned after the Divine Family. God the Father, God the only begotten Son of God, God the Holy Spirit are a family of three. I am not thinking of a family genetically bonded, but spiritually bonded. All ages of spiritual maturity can relate to God's love made manifest, and to family bonds patterned after the Divine Family.

God's administrative order in the Home and in Worship are addressed in the following treatise on The Will of God.

The more knowledgeable one is of the Scriptures, the greater will be the revelation of God's love for one. It will touch one deeply when one learns of the personal sacrifices made by the Father and by the Son, two personalities acting spontaneously in perfect accord to man's tragic circumstance. They had but one objective: the redemption of man, the closing of the breach between God and man caused by sin. The personal sacrifices made by the Father and the Son to redeem fallen man are infinite in character, are everlasting. They are expressive of God's essential being, and make manifest God's love to the uttermost. The redemption of man is the theme of the Bible. It is the foundation upon which God builds His kingdom. The revelation God is giving of Himself is a progressive unveiling to one as he reads and rereads the Bible.

Man is a created personality; can exercise free agency; is responsible and accountable for the choices he makes. Man was created flawless; was in a state of innocence, but was vulnerable to temptation. He was constituted to be complete in a living bond to God, a life sustained by faith, faith motivated by love for God.

There is no way that fallen man can directly relate to the life God was sharing with Adam. In his pristine innocence, there would have been no awesome fear of God in Adam's heart, but trustful reverence in the spirit of worship, the only communion he knew. His delight in pleasing God would have been kindred in spirit to Jesus' delight in pleasing the Father: "I do always those things that please Him" (John 8:29).

God put Adam in the garden to dress it and to keep it. He was occupied in stewardship and in tune with God. Within this paradise of spiritual accord, "The Lord God commanded the man, saying, 'Of every tree in the garden thou mayest freely eat, but of the tree of the knowledge of good and evil, thou shalt not eat of it: for in the day that thou eatest thereof thou shalt surely die'" (Gen. 2:16-17). Adam's life was lived in communion with God in the spirit of worship. No doubt God had often given Adam directional guidance as a father gives his son. Commands made in a spiritual relationship are positive precepts and may carry a warning for infraction that would be consequential, but not a threatening of a penal judgment which would make it legal in character. The precept and the warning were locked in Adam's mind, and he later shared the word of God with Eve.

The garden was Adam's domain of stewardship. Whatever was commanded by God would have been purely objective in Adam's mind. Within this context of spiritual harmony, God was not putting a legal leverage on Adam for obedience or threatening punishment for disobedience.

The commandment God gave to Adam was spiritual in character, not legal; was a positive precept, not a conditional proposal. Adam's life with God subsisted by faith and not by works. "My son, give me thine heart" (Prov. 23:26). Adam was kindred in spirit with God. All of his thoughts and actions would have been in keeping with the character of God.

"And the Lord God said, 'it is not good that the man should be alone, I will make him an help meet for him" (Gen. 2:18). God took from man and made a woman. The twain became one flesh, one entity, two personalities spiritually bonded to God and to each other, genetically constituted to bring forth after their kind. The family life of man, the home, was instituted by God to bear the image of the Divine family.

The world of nature was Adam's domain in which he shared his life with Eve. The warmth of God's love for them endeared God to their hearts. The freedom they enjoyed was consequential to being as God created them to be, bearing His image and sharing His life.

The command given Adam in the garden, and later shared with Eve, was a positive precept whereby their vulnerability to temptation could be tested. A test of their faith in their flawless state would have been without meaning. All of fallen manhood will be tested in some way.

The only way that Adam or Eve could have been tempted to sin would have been in circumstances in which they were unaware of inordinate behavior. God tempts no man to evil. Temptation would have had to have come from outside the camp of God, by an avenging spirit who could not strike at God directly, but strike at the image of God.

"That old serpent, called the Devil and Satan, which deceiveth the whole world; he was cast out into the earth, and his angels were cast out with him" (Rev. 12:9). He was filled with enmity and design when he stealthily entered the garden of Eden. Eve was his target and his prey, his surest way to Adam. He greeted her with a question, a subtle and sure way to engage another in conversation. His question, by intent, cast a doubt on the subject addressed, but was foiled by the word of God readily quoted by Eve. With enticing words and with greater subtlety, he directed her thoughts to something with which she could relate, and with God's blessing. There would have been no self-serving thoughts in Eve's heart as she entertained the words of the Serpent, or in Adam's heart as he stood by. All of their thoughts would have been in keeping with the character of God. I remind my reader that both Adam and Eve were in their flawless state and would have been until they sinned. The depraved mind cannot relate to man in his flawless state, thus is prone to judge them falsely.

The only direct account of the fall of man is contained in one sentence: "she took of the fruit thereof, and did eat, and gave also unto her husband with her; and he did eat" (Gen. 3:6). The eyes of both of them were suddenly opened to their shame. They suffered a spiritual kind of death as they related to God, lost to the life God was sharing with them.

Cross-references to the fall of man simply say that Eve was deceived, that Adam was not deceived (1 Tim. 2:14), and that "by one man's disobedience many were made sinners" (Rom. 5:19). The brief account of the fall of man gives only room for conjecture on the subject. When conjecture is made, and open to challenge, it can be constructive in establishing the whole truth.

It is adjudged because Eve believed the words of the Serpent, she didn't believe the word of God. I have come to see that this is not a logical deduction. More than likely, my readers are Christians. I might ask of one, "Do you believe in the word of God?" In all probability the answer would be, "Yes." Then I would ask, "Have you ever been disobedient to the word of God?" Obviously, the answer would be, "Yes." "For there is no man which sinneth not" (2 Chron. 6:36). Then I would ask, "Was your disobedience unbelief in the word of God?" Conclusively, the answer would be, "No." Disobedience can stem from unbelief, and it is easy for fallen manhood to relate to this possibility, but it cannot be equated with unbelief. All disobedience is sin, but not necessarily unbelief. All will suffer the consequences of sin, both the repentant and the unrepentant. This does not mean that all are condemned. Only the unbelievers are condemned.

Being flawless, Eve's rationale would have been ordinate. The fact that she was beguiled would have made her offense against God inadvertent, but no less disobedient to the command given by God. Eve, as natural as life itself between husband and wife, ate of the fruit and handed the fruit to Adam and he did eat. They ate together for the last time in their innocence. "In the day that thou eatest thereof thou shalt surely die" (Gen. 2:17). They were victims of circumstance, but no less guilty of sin.

No one can judge another's motivations with any degree of certainty. Satan, in the spirit of anti-Christ, would have been enlisting the trust of Eve as a con-man enlists the trust of a rich widow. In her innocence, his words must have seemed reasonable to her. She believed a lie. It is a logical conclusion that she was deluded by his words. The Scriptures say she was deceived. The Scriptures make no reference to unbelief in the heart of Eve or of Adam.

In the minds of some, Adam has been charged with unbelief as the underlying cause of the fall of man. I can no longer accommodate my thinking to this charge. Since the Scriptures do not charge Adam with unbelief, but with disobedience, a reasonable deduction would be that it was a lapse. One can have a lapse from following a positive precept and it be wholly without motivation.

Momentarily, one can have a lapse, be disengaged from what one is doing. Preoccupation of mind may keep one from hearing, seeing, or even from following directions. I might ask someone, "Did you hear that?" He might answer, "No, I didn't hear it." By deduction, I might say, "You are deaf." He would retort, "No, I am not deaf, I just didn't hear it." One cannot accuse Adam of unbelief in his disobedience any more than one can accuse the one who didn't hear of being deaf. Since the Scriptures do not address any motivation of Adam's sin, a safe conclusion is to reckon Adam's sin the consequence of a lapse. There is no motivation in a lapse, but one is responsible for whatever happens while in a lapse. Adam, in his lapse, was disobedient to the command God had given him, and he suffered the consequences.

The consequence of a lapse can be very serious and possibly involve others. It may be more than a casual matter. Lapses of minor consequence happen so often, it isn't easy for one to transpose his thoughts to a lapse of major consequences, like that of Adam's. The church fathers, in their writings, often made reference to the lapse of Adam and Eve.

I can recall an incident that happened over eighty-four years ago. It may sound trivial in the context, but in the circumstance of my dear mother, it wasn't. We were riding on a train, probably the first time for me. When the conductor entered our coach, collecting tickets, Mama handed my ticket to me with definite instructions to hold it until the conductor asked for it. I was sitting on the window side. The window was wide open. The breeze on my face, the motion of the coach, the clickety-clack of the wheels over the rails, and the outlook on the farms we passed intrigued me. I was so carried away, I inadvertently tore up my ticket and threw it out the window. When the conductor asked for our tickets, I didn't have mine. I suddenly realized what I had done. Mama was aggravated at me and upset. To her it meant buying another ticket. The conductor was doing his job, and wasn't too sympathetic. I have no memory of what mama said to me. It was that disciplinary look at such times that I will never forget. I loved and respected her so very much. My lapse, even in my depraved nature, was as inadvertent as Adam's was in his innocence.

The consequences of any lapse are inescapable. Adam suffered a spiritual kind of death and a depraved nature, but was the subject of God's mercy as is all of fallen manhood. (See Appendix A.)

Part II
The Fall and Redemption of Man

It is profitable to reflect on Scripture addressing comparable situations happening possibly years apart. There is something to learn from history that repeats itself. One can discern how vulnerable he can be to reasoning in like circumstances, even with the word of God in mind. I am thinking of Eve, in what is recorded of her in Genesis, chapter three, and of Sarah in Genesis, chapter sixteen, some two thousand years later.

In Genesis, chapter fifteen, it is recorded that God promised Abraham an heir from his own bowels. It was a time in his life when He was already aging. God gave surety to Abraham in a dream: an affirmation of the covenant of promise made with him. Sarah is not mentioned in this chapter. However, from what follows in chapter sixteen, one would know that Abraham had shared the word of God with Sarah, as Adam had with Eve.

Genesis, chapter sixteen, begins with Sarah. Some ten years had passed since the promise of an heir was made to Abraham. Sarah was pondering the word of God. She reasoned logically: if an heir was to be born out of Abraham's bowels, it would have to be from one in his own household who was not barren. "It ceased to be with Sarah after the manner of woman" (Gen. 18:11). In the context of her reasoning, her thinking was logical and her plan not uncommon to her day. She tailored her thoughts on the subject to fit her plan, much like proving a doctrine from the Scriptures, but from Scripture quoted out of context. It can be very effective in proving one's point of view and yet not be the truth.

When the word of God is a consideration in one's thinking, reasoning can be misleading and, when shared, can inadvertently make another a victim of circumstances. Abraham hearkened to the voice of Sarah. He went in unto Hagar, Sarah's maid, and she conceived.

It was not until Sarah lived for a time with the consequence of her plan that she realized her wrong. Then she said to Abraham, "My wrong be upon thee" (Gen. 16:5). He had gone along with his wife's reasoning and now suffered the same consequence. They had Ishmael on their hands. It was not Sarah's intent to deceive Abraham.

From what is recorded, Sarah, Abraham, and Hagar were victims of circumstances. Motivation determines the spiritual value of all personal acts. Only God knows the heart. God did not rebuke them; however, they lived with the consequences.

What is recorded in Genesis, chapter sixteen, of Sarah's reasoning as she contemplated the word of God, and her involvement of Abraham by sharing with him her wrong, seems to be a repeat of history. Earlier in Genesis, chapter three, in the account of the temptation of Eve and the fall of man, there is much similarity. Sarah's wrong shared with Abraham is comparable to Eve's wrong shared with Adam. Both succumbed to what seemed to be logical and reasonable to them. The warfare between Satan and the Seed of the woman, initiated by Eve's encounter with Satan, was expanded by Sarah's wrong in having been a party to Hagar bearing Ishmael, initiating a worldwide conflict—the Judeo-Christian world versus the Islamic world.

It may be that the accounting of Sarah's wrong is good reason for giving a more careful study to what happened in the case of Eve's encounter with Satan. The truth probably lies within their similarity. From what is written, there is no evidence of rebellion against God in either. It is reasonable to think that it is a further unveiling of revelation. What was entailed, and the tragic consequences universally felt, were more than coincidental. We come to a knowledge of the truth by comparing the spiritual with the spiritual, Scripture with Scripture (1 Corin. 2:13). The Bible is the best commentary on the Bible that we have. Cross-references are invaluable.

Eve was fortified by knowledge of the word of God when she was confronted by Satan. His question, "Yea, hath God said, ye shall not eat of every tree in the garden?" (Gen. 3:1) was probably the most subtle means of opening Eve's thinking for him to challenge. She quoted the word of God shared with her by Adam. In her innocence she was in full accord with God. It would not have been likely for her to have had any understanding of the contents of evil, only good. She knew God. In listening to another, one usually hears that with which one can relate. All else only fuels the imagination. However, the commandment had come through clearly enough for her to have dispelled any thought of even touching the tree.

Satan at once addressed the subject of the consequence, something to which she could not directly relate. She was no match for this Goliath. She couldn't possibly have conceived the thought of being lost to the life God was sharing with her. Her feeling of security didn't make death or being lost from a living bond to God relevant. His lead statement, "Ye shall not surely die" (Gen. 3:4), invited a listening ear. Words that suggest a likeness to one's own thinking are disarming and promote further interest. The serpent's reasoning directly followed his lead statement: "For God doth know that in the day ye eat thereof, then your eyes shall be opened, and ye shall be as gods" (Gen. 3:5). He was enticing her with the same ambitious thoughts and objectives he had when he was cast from heaven. He aspired to be like God in power but not in character, not in moral likeness. This part of his reasoning was not of relevance to Eve. She was created in the image of God, was bearing His likeness and was enjoying being as she was created: flawless, in tune with God, with Adam, and with all of natural creation. All actions stemming from her heart would have been motivated by love. She knew only good. Evil was not a reckoning influence as it is to fallen man.

The Apostle John in the Book of Revelation clearly identifies the serpent: "And the great dragon was cast out, that old serpent, called the Devil, and Satan, which deceiveth the whole world: he was cast out into the earth, and his angels were cast out with him" (Rev. 12:9). He still has the power of deception with which man must reckon. "We wrestle not against flesh and blood, but against spiritual wickedness in high places" (Eph. 6:12).

In Satan's reasoning with Eve, the Hebrew word "Elohim" is translated "gods": "Ye shall be as gods" (Gen. 3:5). She knew only the one God, the true and living God. She was in direct communion with Him, a living identity to which Satan could not relate. In no way could Eve have accommodated her thinking to this translation. She could have related to the phrase had it been translated, "Ye shall be like God," not to aspire for power, but to be like God in whose image she was created.

It may be of interest to note that this is the only place in the Book of Genesis the Hebrew word "Elohim" is translated in the plural, "gods." This was the one time out of some two hundred times it occurs. "The form of Elohim is plural, but the construction is uniformly singular, and governs a singular verb or adjective, unless used of heathen divinities (reference I.S.B.E.—*International Standard Bible Encyclopedia*). In the Hebrew language, the plural is often used to express the superlative, as in, "In the beginning Elohim (translated God) created the heavens and the earth" (Gen. 1:1). Creation was by the wisdom and power of the one and only true God, not by gods. The phrase, "Ye shall be as gods," as quoted above, was translated, "Ye shall be like God," in the Syriac Version, a very early version. The translation, "Ye shall be as gods," is expressive of Satan's ambitions for power, but translated in the plural would not have been relevant to Eve's identity with the true and living God.

It comes natural to one who is responsive to God's love for him to want to be like Him in character, and to be found pleasing to Him. A Christian can relate to this in wanting to be like Jesus. The Apostle Paul said, "The love of Christ constraineth us" (2 Cor. 5:14). Think of how much more this would have been true of Eve, who knew no sin.

It wasn't until Satan began using the rationale of ordinate desires that his subtlety became effective. Natural desires, before sin, could have been satisfied with the blessing of God. Eve had taken note that the fruit of the tree was attractive and edible, probably similar to other trees in the garden. Her desire to gain knowledge is commendable.

"She took of the fruit thereof and did eat and gave also unto her husband with her, and he did eat" (Gen. 3:6). No dialogue between them on the subject is recorded. To read motivation in the context would be pure conjecture. She gave to her husband to eat as innocently as Sarah involved Abraham. She was not deceiving Adam. She was the one who was deceived, not Adam (1 Tim. 2:14). It would have been perfectly natural for him to have eaten food handed him by his wife. He was implicated in circumstances much like Abraham was with Sarah. He was made a party to Eve's wrong, and they shared the consequences together.

The precept, "But of the tree of the knowledge of good and evil, thou shalt not eat of it" (Gen. 2:17), was understandable to them. They could relate to what He was saying. It was a positive precept directional in Character—a situation wherein God gave Adam and Eve latitude to exercise their free agency in the face of their vulnerability to temptation. God was not testing their faith. A test of their faith in their flawless state would have been without meaning. Only they knew to what the precept had reference, and had been warned of the consequence of disobedience, but it was something to which they could not relate. (See Appendix B.)

God had said, "For in the day thou eatest thereof thou shalt surely die." The day Adam and Eve sinned, they were lost to a living bond to God. It was consequential and not a judgment of God on sin. They suffered a personal or spiritual loss, not penal in character. They were not being punished. They were lost to the life God was sharing with them. They were literally divorced from a living bond to God. Their betrothal to God was broken. They were created to be complete in a living bond to God. Now they suffered a spiritual kind of death as they related to God.

The conscience is like a built-in censor; it is innate in one's personality. It is easy as long as one is at peace with God, but triggers guilt when one sins. The closer one is to God the more sensitive is his conscience. When Adam and Eve sinned, their conscience condemned them. They felt the sting of death. They were afraid and tried to hide from God. Nobody can.

God had compassion on them and called to them. Sin distances one from God, but they heard His voice. They were subjects of God's mercy. He did not rebuke them. They were victims of circumstance. Eve had been beguiled; and she subsequently involved Adam and Adam's posterity. All of manhood suffers the consequence of their sin. All are born in a spiritual kind of death as they relate to God; redemption unto a spiritual kind of life is made secure by one's faith in Jesus, faith motivated by a responsive love to God's love.

"For as in Adam all die, even so in Christ shall all be made alive" (1 Cor. 15:22). All were in the loins of Adam when Adam sinned. The Son of God incarnate had no posterity in His loins. All believers by adoption make up the family of God.

Adam and Eve responded to God's query and told it as it was. Their confession was forthright and brief. Before pronouncing any judgment (they were already suffering a personal loss as a consequence of their sin), God gave them hope in promising them life: the restoration of a living bond to Himself through faith in the Seed of the woman. The judgments that followed were on their respective offices and terminated with time, a curse that affected the stewardship of all women and men.

The day Adam and Eve sinned, they suffered the death that God before had warned would happen. The promise of redemption from death unto life was likewise effected the day they believed in the promised Seed, the Savior.

It is in the minds of many Christians that if Adam and Eve had not eaten of the tree of the knowledge of good and evil, they would have lived forever. This would not only have made eternal life a reward of merit, but also a contradiction to having been created with mortal bodies.

"The Lord God formed man of the dust of the ground and breathed into his nostrils the breath of life; and man became a living soul" (Gen. 2:7). All of Adam's posterity was in his loins. "All flesh shall perish together, and man shall turn again to dust" (Job 34:15). "Flesh and blood cannot inherit the kingdom of God" (1 Cor. 15:50). The bodies of Adam and Eve were mortal. Mortal man is a creature of time, and like all creatures of time, has a life cycle. "There is a time to be born and a time to die" (Eccles. 3:1-2). Adam lived 930 years and died. His mortal death was not a judgment of God on sin, but the way of all flesh. Had Adam been created with an immortal body, he would not have been subject to death. Our Lord, in assuming manhood, was made like unto His brethren. He assumed a mortal body: "A body hast thou prepared me," (Heb. 10:5). As our file leader, the mortal took on immortality, giving us surety or vouchsafing the redemption of the whole man, body and spirit. The believer has this hope.

The mortal death of Jesus couldn't have been a judgment of God on sin. He was without sin. There is no way that one can suffer the personal consequences of another's sin vicariously, any more than one can transfer qualities of character by legacy.

All theories are framed in known truth together with suppositions of the truth. A supposition proven faulty is supplanted by that which is more likely to be the truth. This not only strengthens the theory, but also gives it greater credibility.

An atonement for sin to reconcile God to man is basic to the Judeo-Christian worship of God. The means whereby an atonement has been made has been given support by many differing theories. The vicarious theory is most widely held. The faith theory of the atonement is a challenge to the truth of the vicarious theory. It is the legal premise upon which the vicarious theory of the atonement is built that is being challenged. A spiritual objective cannot be directly accomplished by legal means. The vicarious theory is too licensing to be the whole truth. Any spiritual value coming from it would have to be indirect. The faith theory of the atonement is built on a spiritual premise and addresses only that which relates to one's person. Sin causes one to suffer a personal loss (affects one's spiritual stature), not a legal judgment, (is not punitive in character). All that is accruing to one's spiritual stature in time will determine the degree of celestial glory or of damnation one will live with in eternity. The judgment our Lord will make of one in eternity will be an affirmation of what has already taken place in time. It is sobering to know one is charting one's own destiny. (See Appendix C.)

Part III
The Fall and Redemption of Man

Consequential to the lapse of Adam and Eve, all of fallen manhood is suffering a spiritual kind of death as each relates to God, a depraved nature, and a curse. The former losses are personal in character and the latter impersonal. The personal losses have been addressed earlier in this treatise.

God decreed a curse, first on the woman and then on the man. It affected them in the execution of their respective offices, making their stewardship more laborious. The curse was not a personal matter; it applied to all women and to all men down through time. It was decreed by the wisdom of God and for the good of manhood. It would be a constant reminder to man of his dependence on God and of the consequences of sin.

All of fallen manhood is in a depraved state: the intellect, the emotions, the will, and the conscience are all functionally impaired. One can be no more than wholly depraved, but one's personal stature can be more corrupt than another's as a consequence of sinning.

Fallen man is no less responsible, can make choices, and is accountable for his acts. He didn't lose what is inherent in man. Man has an innate proclivity Godward; is instinctively conscious of being incomplete apart from God; and has a conscience that addresses man's moral actions. One has to clear all of these hurdles in order to avoid thoughts of God.

Fallen man needs to be redeemed from a spiritual kind of death, as he relates to God, unto a spiritual kind of life. Before the fall, the life God was sharing with man was sustained by faith. Disobedience created the breach. Since faith and disobedience are spiritual in character, the only logical conclusion is that the breach must be closed by spiritual means, which would be by the obedience of a sinless man, as man was sinless before the breach. This prerequisite disqualifies all of fallen manhood. As death reigns from the disobedience of one man, the first Adam, so life reigns from the obedience of the last Adam, Jesus Christ, obedience motivated by love for God. He closed the breach and reconciled God to man. The Gospel invites man to be reconciled to God through faith in Jesus Christ, faith motivated by love for God.

God can be reconciled to man only as God created him to be, manhood in a living bond to God. Reconciliation is spiritual in character. It is the restoring of a spiritual or personal relationship to what it was before the breach was made, but in the new birth the life of the believer is secure in Christ, security Adam and Eve didn't have. Reconciliation is much more than making peace with God. It is literally laying down one's life for God as God laid down His life for man, creating a living bond, a marriage, motivated by a responsive love to God's love. In my day, the United States is at peace with Russia, but not reconciled. They are poles apart in their ideology. Peace can be made on legal terms, but not reconciliation. Jacob made peace with Esau, but they were never reconciled.

We know from what is written that Adam and Eve were reconciled to God. They believed God when God gave them hope of redemption through faith in the Seed of the woman. Adam made a confession of their faith with Eve in the following quote: "Adam called his wife's name Eve; because she was the mother of all living" (Gen. 3:20), as Abraham is the father of the children of faith (Gal. 3:7).

The reconciliation of God to man and of man to God was first revealed to Adam and Eve in a ritual of worship officiated by God. "The Lord God made coats of skins, and clothed them" (Gen. 3:21). This could have been a theophany, an appearance of God prefiguring in type the living sacrifice the Son of God made of Himself to redeem man and to clothe him in the garments of salvation. This is purely conjecture. All that is known for a certainty is that they got the message. What would have been instinctive in their worship of God before the fall, was now given direction from God in rituals of worship for them and their posterity to observe until what was prefigured in type was fulfilled in the Seed of the woman, in Jesus Christ.

God revealed Himself through the rituals of worship ordained by Him and officiated by an expanding priesthood of His appointment: first to the head over his own family, which would have been Adam, and to all successive heads over their respective families. Headship was given to the man with the enablement to execute his office. The priesthood over his family was never abrogated, but made subject to the priesthood over collective families, like tribal or kindred entities: for example, Jethro, the priest of Midian. It was in his day, that Israel, in covenant identity with God, became a theocratic nation, and, by the election of God, an expanded priesthood, a witness to all peoples of the true and living God. The history of Israel in the making was a progressive unveiling of the revelation of God in circumstances with which all of manhood can relate: promises made and fulfilled, prophecy foretold and come to pass time and time again—building the credibility of the word of God in the hearts of all peoples.

After the promises made to Abraham, Isaac, and Jacob were fulfilled in the coming of the promised One, God expanded His priesthood once more from a national priesthood under the Old Covenant to a universal priesthood under the New Covenant. At Pentecost, the Holy Spirit was given to quicken all believers into a spiritual or living entity, the Body of Christ, which today finds embodiment in local churches the world over.

The rituals of worship were a spiritual communique from God, and, like a universal language, carried the same message of God's redeeming love to all peoples. The message was made effectual by the Holy Spirit to all who had hearts for God, creating a responsive love to God's love for them.

Adam was a faithful steward to God in his priestly ministry to his family. It was his responsibility to officiate worship as directed by God. The time of his worship was no doubt the Sabbath Day. He taught the message of God's redeeming love; officiated the rites of worship; and lived an exemplary life motivated by love for God.

Cain and Abel sat under the priesthood of their own father, as did Shem, Ham, and Japheth several hundred years later. The responses given were as they are today under like ministry. They are either legal (impersonal) or spiritual (personal) in character. One may not fully understand the difference between the legal and the spiritual.

The legal is always motivated by self-interests. There is no giving of oneself in a legal response or involvement. It is observing the rites of worship as one has been taught, and resting in what he has done to make him acceptable to God—observing formal worship, doing what is required of one, keeping covenant, and the like. Apart from a personal involvement with God, the above are legal in character, and are in some way self-serving.

A spiritual or personal response is an exercise of faith, motivated by love for God, and executed in the spirit of worship. One literally gives of one's self to God, and to God's glory. Consequently, a larger place is being made in one's heart for God. A living bond to God subsists by spiritual means, by faith motivated by love for God. All responses to the contrary are self-serving, are spiritually negative.

The offerings of Cain and Abel in their worship of God contrast the legal and the spiritual. Cain's offering was legal in character and Abel's spiritual. Both Cain and Abel brought first fruit offerings unto God, of the yields from their respective fields of labor. Either one would have been bothered not to have heeded conscience in following the forms of worship they had been taught from their youth, even if their hearts were not in it. Only from what is written can one discern why Abel's offering was acceptable to God and Cain's wasn't. However, cross-references further reveal what is obvious in the context. Cain's works were evil, and his brother's righteous. "For this is the message that ye heard from the beginning, that we should love one another. Not as Cain, who was of that wicked one, and slew his brother. And wherefore slew he him? Because his own works were evil, and his brother's righteous" (1 John 3:11-12).

"Unto Cain and to his offering He had not respect" (Gen. 4:5). Cain's worship was not offered in spirit and in truth. He gave of the first fruits of his land an offering unto God, but not of himself. His worship was self-serving, was not motivated by love for God. For one to worship in form while hating his brother would have been impersonal in character; his heart would not have been in his worship. Cain's unrighteous spirit surfaced in his wrath. God's omniscience, knowing the heart of Cain, didn't affect His compassion for Cain as He reasoned with him. When one and one's offering are unacceptable to God, sin lieth at the door. It was a personal problem with Cain that could not be resolved by impersonal or legal means. There must be a personal identity with the redeemer for one's worship to be acceptable to God.

"And the Lord had respect unto Abel and to his offering" (Gen. 4:4). "By faith Abel offered unto God a more excellent sacrifice than Cain, by which he obtained witness that he was righteous, God testifying of his gifts" (Heb. 11:4). Abel's offering bore witness that he was redeemed—was in a living bond to God. First fruit offerings were an acknowledgment of God's bountiful provision. However,

Abel's offering was more inclusive, in that he offered himself, a living sacrifice, in identity with a living sacrifice that prefigured the Lamb of God in type. He was observing the burnt offering or love offering as ordained by God.

There was a difference to God between the sacrifices offered by Cain and by Abel that made one of them and his offering acceptable and the other one not. Abel offered a more excellent sacrifice than Cain simply because his heart was in his worship. He gave of himself in identity with the Lamb of God in the rituals of worship he observed. Without one's heart being in worship of God, there is a wanting of spiritual value. The Apostle Paul says it this way, "Bodily exercise profiteth little: but godliness is profitable unto all things, having promise of the life that now is, and of that which is to come" (1 Tim. 4:8). There is always hope for one who observes family worship or the worship of collective families. One is within the range of hearing the word of God.

The rituals of worship observed by the fathers in patriarchal times would have been offered in typology that prefigured in type the offering of oneself in identity with the Lamb of God, and motivated by love for God in spirit. At intervals of time, the lives of certain holy men of God are of record. Their offerings, and the spirit in which they were offered, bear witness that they were justified—were in a living bond to God as God created man to be. They had received the message of God's redeeming love.

Noah was the tenth patriarch descended from Adam in the line of the Seed. Noah's day was centuries after Cain and Abel, but the same contrast in the spirit of worship prevailed in the hearts of man. Man's wickedness was great on the earth. The Lord repented that He had made man. He told Noah that He would destroy man from the face of the earth, but Noah found grace in the eyes of the Lord. He believed God and was obedient to his calling. Noah was a preacher of righteousness. His message would have been with personal conviction and compassion. In no way was he trying to get people saved from the flood, but from condemnation. His plea would have been for them to have believed God and to have lived to God's glory. Those of Noah's posterity were the generations of a new world.

Abraham lived some five hundred years or more after Noah. He also had gotten the message. The promised One was revelation to Abraham in his day. Our Lord said to the Jews, "'Your father Abraham rejoiced to see my day: and he saw it, and was glad.' Then said the Jews unto him, 'Thou art not yet fifty years old, and hast thou seen Abraham?' Jesus said unto them, 'Verily, verily, I say unto you, Before Abraham was, I am'" (John 8:56-58). Who, better than Abraham, would have been one to whom the Jews could have related? Today, it would be like getting God's message of redemption from the Bible. There are still those who do not believe.

Abraham must have had two calls from God (Acts 7:2-3). The first was to get out of the country of the Chaldeans, to leave Ur of the Chaldees. Abraham's family and his father Terah and family left with him and settled in Haran, still in the country of Mesopotamia. For a family to pull stakes and travel together at a call from God was revealing of being kindred in spirit and in family bonds. They had moved under God's directions, to an area open to be possessed. Laban literally became a land baron: his holdings reached as far as Padamaram which was later known as Laban's city. The area around Haran became a dwelling place for Terah and his posterity. This was shown later when Abraham didn't want his son, Isaac, to marry a Canaanite. He sent his servant, Eliezer, to the land of his kindred, of his father's house, to seek a bride for Isaac. The same concern was in the heart of Isaac for his son, Jacob. He didn't want Jacob to marry a Canaanite and sent him to Haran, to the house of Laban, to seek a wife from his own people.

The second call to Abraham was to leave his father's house "unto a land that I will show thee: and I will make of thee a great nation, and I will bless thee, and make thy name great; and thou shalt be a blessing" (Gen. 12:1-2). Abraham was seventy-five years old. He was obedient to the call of God and departed as the Lord had spoken to him. He took Sarah, his wife, and Lot, his brother's son, and all their substance and souls they had gotten in Haran to go forth unto the land of Canaan. As they journeyed, wherever he pitched tent he built an altar unto the Lord and worshipped.

Abraham lived in the spirit of worship and in communion with God. The Lord said of Abraham, "For I know him, that he will command his children and his household after him, and they shall keep the way of the Lord, to do justice and judgment; that the Lord may bring upon Abraham that which he hath spoken of him" (Gen. 18:19).

Abraham's steadfast faith and his love for God was also exemplified in the life of his son, Isaac, and in his grandson, Jacob. The only true and living God was known to generations to come as the God of Abraham, Isaac, and Jacob.

Abraham's name is probably the best known in the religious world. The three great monotheistic religions stem from him: Islam, Judaism, and Christianity.

God tried Abraham in circumstances to prove his faith, love, and obedience. Time and again when God called to Abraham, the quick response was, "Behold, here I am." There was no guile in him; his life was an open book to God. And God said, "'Take now thy son, thine only son Isaac, whom thou lovest, and get thee into the land of Moriah; and offer him there for a burnt offering upon one of the mountains which I will tell thee of.' And Abraham rose up early in the morning, and saddled his ass, and took two of his young men with him, and Isaac, his son, and clave the wood for the burnt offering, and went unto the place of which God had told him. Then on the third day Abraham lifted up his eyes, and saw the place afar off. And Abraham said unto his young men, 'Abide ye here with the ass; and I and the lad will go yonder and worship, and come again to you'" (Gen. 22:2-5).

Isaac, no doubt, had gone with his father many times to build altars and offer burnt offerings unto God. The rituals of worship, ordained by God, were not only well known to him, but meaningful in type. "And Isaac spake unto Abraham his father, and said, 'My father:' and he said, 'Here am I, my son.' And he said, 'Behold the fire and the wood: but where is the lamb for a burnt offering?' And Abraham said, 'My son, God will provide himself a lamb for a burnt offering:' so they went both of them together" (Gen. 22:7-8). Their mutual faith in God bonded them to each other. Isaac didn't live in the shadow of his father, but up front with his father. It takes spiritual accord for two to walk together as they did. They had but a single objective, to walk with God, never doubting.

Isaac, according to Josephus, was twenty-six years old, but was in his early thirties by some chronologists. He would have been in the prime of his youth. Abraham was over 125 years of age.

There would have been no way for him to have outmuscled Isaac to have bound him, had he resisted. What affects one personally is not considered in the exercise of faith motivated by love for God.

"And Abraham stretched forth his hand, and took the knife to slay his son. And the angel of the Lord called unto him out of heaven, and said, 'Abraham, Abraham:' and he said, 'Here am I.' And he said, 'Lay not thine hand upon the lad, neither do thou anything unto him: for now I know that thou fearest God, seeing thou has not withheld thy son, thine only son from me.' And Abraham lifted up his eyes, and looked, and behold behind him a ram caught in a thicket by his horns: and Abraham went and took the ram, and offered him up for a burnt offering in the stead of his son" (Gen. 22:10-13).

The offering of Isaac, in the ritual of worship ordained by God, would have been unacceptable to God—a departure from typology. Isaac was a depraved man—less than perfect. God provided the perfect offering, the ram, prefiguring in type the Lamb of God. Abraham took the ram, and offered him up for a burnt offering in the stead of Isaac. The ram took Isaac's place in the ritual of worship as ordained by God, but not Isaac's place in his worship of God. No one can take another's place in the worship of God. The ritual of the burnt offering, officiated by Abraham, was the offering of themselves, living sacrifices to God, in identity with the perfect One in type.

After having worshipped, they returned to the young men as Abraham had said. They were totally unmindful of having passed the acid test of their faith.

God often repeated His promises to Abraham, not as reassurance to him, but so that all peoples could build their faith and hope. Credibility is built upon the fulfillment of promises made. The blessings of God upon Abraham, Isaac, and Jacob bear witness to God's hand on their lives. The altars of worship they built and the sacrifices they offered are expressive of the spirit of worship that was resident in their hearts.

Abraham, when stricken in age, sent his eldest servant, Eliezer, to Mesopotamia, to his own kindred, to take a wife for his son, Isaac. The line of his posterity was of concern to him, simply because it kept the line of the Seed in the family of Abraham. By providential circumstances, the Lord led Eliezer directly to Rebekah, the daughter of Bethuel, the son of Nahor, Abraham's brother.

Isaac was forty years old when he and Rebekah were married, and sixty years old when she gave birth to Esau and Jacob, twins. Isaac had entreated the Lord for Rebekah, because she was barren. It was through his genes that his seed would be of the posterity of Abraham. Esau was born first, but it was Jacob who had spiritual discernment and a heart for God. Esau, to satisfy an insatiable appetite, sold his birthright to Jacob for bread and a pottage of lentils. He ate, drank, and rose up to pursue his self-serving life: thus he despised his birthright. Jacob, through his subtlety, was none the richer. One's birthright is not a marketable commodity. No one can transfer one's personal heritage or spiritual status to another.

When Isaac was old and his eyes dim, he asked Esau, his eldest son, to prepare "savory meat such as I love . . ., that my soul may bless thee before I die" (Gen. 27:4). Jacob, in subtlety, intercepted the blessing. Esau said to his father, "Is not he rightly named Jacob? for he hath supplanted me these two times: he took away my birthright; and, behold, now he hath taken away my blessing" (Gen. 27:36). Esau hated Jacob, and was of a mind to kill him. Upon hearing this, Rebekah asked Jacob to obey her and flee to Laban, her brother in Haran, "until thy brother's fury turn away" (Gen. 27:44). Timely to the situation at hand, she complained to Isaac of her life being made weary because of the daughters of Heth, probably the wives of Esau. Straightforthly, Isaac called Jacob and charged him not to take a wife of the daughters of Canaan. "Arise, go to Padanaram, to the house of Bethuel thy mother's father; and take thee a wife from thence of the daughters of Laban thy mother's brother. And God Almighty bless thee, and make thee fruitful, and multiply thee, that thou mayest be a multitude of people; and give thee the blessing of Abraham, to thee, and to thy seed with thee; that thou mayest inherit the land wherein thou art a stranger, which God gave unto Abraham" (Gen. 28:2-4).

Jacob set out for Haran; at a certain place he tarried all night and dreamed of a ladder set up on earth, "and the top of it reached to heaven: and behold the angels of God ascending and descending on it. And, behold, the Lord stood above it, and said, 'I am the Lord God of Abraham thy father, and the God of Isaac: the land whereon thou liest, to thee will I give it, and to thy seed; and thy seed shall be as the dust of the earth, and thou shalt spread abroad to the west, and to the east, and to the north, and to the south: and in thee and in thy seed shall all the families of the earth be blessed. And, behold, I am with thee, and will keep thee in all places whither thou goest, and will bring thee again into this land; for I will not leave thee, until I have done that which I have spoken to thee of'" (Gen. 28:12-15). Jacob called the name of the place, Bethel, the house of God.

By circumstances of providence, God led him to the house of Laban, his mother's brother. He was given a warm welcome. He fell in love with Rachel upon first sight of her.

After Jacob had stayed with them a month, he had impressed Laban enough for Laban to ask him to serve him for wages. Jacob agreed to serve him seven years for Rachel, his younger daughter. The seven years of his service to Laban were as a few days, he loved her so much. He asked Laban to give Rachel to him to be his wife. The way Laban beguiled him in first giving him his elder daughter, Leah, is well known. Jacob served Laban another seven years for Rachel.

"And Laban said unto him, 'I pray thee, if I have found favour in thine eyes, tarry: for I have learned by experience that the Lord hath blessed me for thy sake'" (Gen. 30:27). Jacob would take nothing from Laban, but agreed to stay on and feed his flock under conditions wherein God could prosper him. Everything he had increased exceedingly. It excited jealousy in the sons of Laban and Laban's countenance was not good toward him. "And the Lord said unto Jacob, 'return unto the land of thy fathers, and to thy kindred; and I will be with thee' . . . And the angel of God spake unto me in a dream, saying, 'Jacob:' And I said, 'Here am I'" (Gen. 31:3,11). God had seen all that Laban had done unto him. Jacob stole away unawares and took with him all he had. It was told to Laban on the third day that Jacob was fled. Laban pursued after him seven days and overtook him. "And God came to Laban the Syrian in a dream by night, and said unto him, 'Take heed that thou speak not to Jacob either good or bad'" (Gen. 31:24). They made peace and parted to go their separate ways.

No sooner had he gotten over this encounter than he learned that his brother, Esau, was coming with four hundred men to meet him. He was afraid and distressed in spirit. He unburdened his heart to God. "And Jacob said, 'O God of my father Abraham, and God of my father Isaac, the Lord which saidst unto me, return unto thy country, and to thy kindred, and I will deal well with thee: I am not worthy of the least of all the mercies, and of all the truth, which thou hast shewed unto thy servant; for with my staff I passed over this Jordan; and now I am become two bands. Deliver me, I pray thee, from the hand of my brother, from the hand of Esau: for I fear him, lest he will come and smite me, and the mother with the children. And thou saidst, I will surely do thee good, and make thy seed as the sand of the sea, which cannot be numbered for multitude'" (Gen. 32:9-12). He sent ahead droves of his live stock, spaced at intervals, as presents for Esau so that peradventure when they met, Esau would accept him. This subtlety was characteristic of Jacob, but one must not be blinded to God's hand on his life. In all that he did, there was no less room for God in his heart or any reproach brought upon God. Obviously, he had a spiritual bond to God that could possibly make others envious, as were Laban's sons.

The night before meeting Esau, Jacob had his two wives and all that he had pass over the ford Jabbok before him—"and Jacob was left alone, and there wrestled a man with him . . . And he said, 'Let me go, for the day breaketh.' And he said, 'I will not let thee go, except thou bless me.' And he said unto him, 'What is thy name?' And he said, 'Jacob.'

And he said, 'Thy name shall be called no more Jacob, but Israel: for as a prince hast thou power with God and with men, and hast prevailed.' And Jacob asked him, and said, 'Tell me, I pray thee, thy name.' And he said, 'Wherefore is it that thou dost ask after my name?' and he blessed him there. And Jacob called the name of the place Peniel: 'for I have seen God face to face, and my life is preserved'" (Gen. 32:24, 26-30).

"And Jacob lifted up his eyes, and looked, and, behold, Esau came, and with him four hundred men" (Gen. 33:1). Jacob was especially protective of Rachel and Joseph, putting them hindermost to his family. He went before them cautiously and bowed himself to the ground seven times, until he came near to his brother. "And Esau ran to meet him, and embraced him, and fell on his neck, and kissed him: and they wept" (Gen. 33:4). After the insistence of Jacob, Esau took of the presents offered. They had made peace, but were never reconciled. That day Esau returned on his way to Seir, and Jacob journeyed toward the land of Canaan.

God told Jacob to go to Bethel and to build an altar unto Him there, where He had appeared to him before, when he fled from the face of Esau, his brother. This time Jacob took his whole household with him to worship God. And God appeared unto Jacob again and blessed him. "And God said unto him, 'thy name is Jacob: thy name shall not be called any more Jacob, but Israel shall be thy name:' and he called his name Israel. And God said unto him, 'I am God Almighty: be fruitful and multiply; a nation and a company of nations shall be of thee, and kings shall come out of thy loins; and the land which I gave Abraham and Isaac, to thee I will give it, and to thy seed after thee will I give the land'" (Gen. 35:10-12).

As they traveled from Bethel, nearing Ephrath, Rachel travailed in hard labor and died in giving birth to Benjamin: he was the only child of Jacob not born in Haran. Jacob was very protective of Joseph and Benjamin, the only two of Jacob's offspring from Rachel. More of Jacob's history is recorded of him before he settled in Canaan, but God was always at his right hand.

The promises of God made to Abraham, Isaac, and Jacob serve as the foundation to God's historical revelation of Himself that culminated in Jesus Christ: in Jesus all the promises of God are fulfilled, and in Him rests the hope of all peoples.

Abraham, Isaac, and Jacob are the progenitors of the line of the Seed, of Jesus Christ. Their lives are a revelation of the abundant life the depraved man can have in a living bond to God under circumstances current in this lifetime. A living bond to God is spiritual in character and is effected by faith, faith motivated by a responsive love to God's love. Love for God will be the prevailing influence in one's life—whatever the circumstances are.

This abundant life issues from a spiritual kind of death wherein love finds expression in the laying down of one's life for another. It was literally exemplified in the offering Abraham made of Isaac, when God stayed Abraham's hand. Figuratively, by faith, Abraham had already received Isaac back from the dead, accounting that God was able to raise him up, even from the dead. He believed God's promise to him, "In Isaac shall thy seed be called" (Gen. 21:12). Only by the imagination can one perceive the closer bonding of their hearts to God as they walked from the altar of worship. (One never lays down as much as one picks up: one picks up the abundant life.) The effects of this interaction are also true when the love of a husband and wife for each other finds expression in the spirit of devotion. It is a quality of life that is inexplainable, simply because it is too personal to articulate in words. It can be observed by others, but never imitated. One will give of oneself to please the one he loves which begets a personal response from the one loved. Both are endeared the more to each other. One who lays down his life for God will see new evidences of God's love for oneself daily. One will be picking up the abundant life—the life God created man to have.

Part IV
The Fall and Redemption of Man

Down through the years, there has been an unbroken chain of men of God who were pillars of light keeping alive the hope of the promises of God to Abraham, Isaac, and Jacob. There was never a time when there wasn't a voice for God in the land.

The sacred history of the life of Joseph is revelation of the only true and living God making ready a place for incubating the nation Israel. If one doesn't see this objective of God in the background of what is written, he will have lost the continuity of God building on His promises to Abraham, Isaac, and Jacob. They were the progenitors of the line of the Seed. The maintaining of the line of the Seed is always relevant in the context of the recorded sacred history.

Jacob was what we would consider an old man when Joseph was born. Jacob's love for God and his fatherly love for Joseph made him a strong influence on Joseph's life. They were kindred in spirit in their relationship to God. This created a spiritual bond between them that excited jealously in the hearts of his older brothers.

Joseph had a premonition from God in a dream. He told his dream to his father and brothers. It incensed his older brothers into hatred—enough to want to get rid of him. Joseph, at the time of his dream, probably didn't know the meaning of it. It would be revelation to all of them when it came to pass—some twenty years later.

Joseph was seventeen years old when, at an opportune time, his brothers sold him to Ishmaelite traders who were in a caravan on their way to Egypt. They, in turn, sold him to Potiphar, an officer of Pharaoh and captain of the guard.

His master saw that the Lord was with Joseph, and that the Lord made all that he did to prosper in his hand. The captain made him overseer of his house and everything he had.

Back in Canaan, Joseph's brothers feigned the possibility of his death to Jacob, who mourned for his son many days, and could not be comforted. He was close to 110 years of age.

Potiphar's wife accused Joseph wrongfully. Joseph's master put him into the prison where Pharaoh's prisoners were bound. The Lord was with Joseph and gave him favor in the eyes of the keeper of the prison, who committed all the prisoners to Joseph's hand. God was giving Joseph timely schooling for more responsible stewardship.

Most of my readers know about Joseph rightly interpreting the dreams of Pharaoh's chief butler and baker, both of whom were held in prison under Joseph's guard. The chief butler was restored to his butlership, but he forgot Joseph until two years later, when Pharaoh had a dream that troubled him in spirit. Not one of the magicians or wise men of Egypt could interpret his dream. The chief butler remembered and told Pharaoh about how Joseph rightfully interpreted the dreams he and the chief baker had while in prison. Pharaoh sent and called for Joseph to be brought to him at once.

Joseph was thirty years old when he stood before Pharaoh, king of Egypt. He interpreted Pharaoh's dream of that which was established by God and would shortly come to pass: of the seven years of plenty in the land and of the seven years of famine which would follow. Joseph addressed the subject of survival. It was all good in the eyes of Pharaoh and his servants. Pharaoh made Joseph prime minister over all of Egypt. God gave wisdom to Joseph in executing his stewardship to Pharaoh.

The famine came as predicted. Only in Egypt was there corn. Jacob, dwelling in Canaan, heard that there was plenty in Egypt and sent Joseph's ten older brothers down to Egypt to buy corn. When Joseph saw his brothers bow down before him and not recognize him, he remembered his dream. I refer my reader to a living drama of sacred history recorded in Genesis, chapters forty-two through forty-five.

Joseph's brothers told Jacob of Joseph's glory, and he said, "I will go and see him before I die" (Gen. 45:28). God told Jacob to fear not to go down into Egypt, "For there will I make of thee a great nation" (Gen. 46:3). Pharaoh gave the good land of Egypt, the land of Goshen, to Joseph for a settling place for the Israelites to dwell and to graze their cattle. Jacob, his family, and his household moved to Egypt, bringing with them their livestock and all that they had.

"And Israel said unto Joseph, 'Behold, I die: but God shall be with you, and bring you again unto the land of your fathers'" (Gen. 48:21). Before he died, he gathered his sons together and told them what would befall them in the last days. What he said to Judah is of special importance because he is in the kingly line of the genealogy of our Lord (Gen. 49:10). Jacob died at the age of 147 years, after having lived in Egypt seventeen years. Joseph died at the age of 110 years.

The nation, Israel, was an embryo in the womb of Egypt, and fared well as long as Joseph was prime minister. God prospered His people: "And the children of Israel were fruitful, and increased abundantly, and multiplied, and waxed exceeding mighty; and the land was filled with them" (Exod. 1:7). They became the envy of the Egyptians.

Generations after Joseph's death, there arose a king over Egypt who knew not Joseph. He championed the spirit of the Egyptians against the Israelites and dealt harshly with them, and made their lives bitter with hard bondage.

Under his reign Moses was born. By providential circumstances Moses was saved from an edict of the king: to cast all males born of the Israelites into the river. By the compassion of Pharaoh's daughter, his life was spared. She paid wages to a Hebrew woman, his mother, to nurse and care for him while growing, and then to bring him to her to be her son. Moses' father and mother were Levites who would have taught him, from the cradle, of the God of Abraham, Isaac, and Jacob. All of his Egyptian schooling didn't alienate him from God and his Hebrew brethren.

When Moses was forty years old, he spied an Egyptian smiting one of his brethren. He slew the Egyptian and hid his body in the sand. When Moses learned that what he had done had become known, he fled to the land of Midian. He married the daughter of Jethro, the priest of Midian, a gentile priest who knew the only true and living God. Moses was content to dwell with him and to tend his flock. Jethro, no doubt, was sharing the revelation of God he had with Moses, a time of schooling by providential circumstances. The rituals of worship he officiated were as God ordained them. Moses sat under the ministry of Jethro for forty years. He was being made ready to respond to a call from God.

While Moses was tending Jethro's flock on the backside of the desert, at the foot of Mount Horeb, God spoke to him from a burning bush. When God said, "I am the God of Abraham, the God of Isaac, and the God of Jacob" (Exod. 3:6), He was not a stranger to Moses, but the only true and living God. God had heard the cry of the children of Israel, and had seen their affliction, which was well known to Moses. "Come now therefore, and I will send thee unto Pharaoh, that thou mayest bring forth my people the children of Israel out of Egypt" (Exod. 3:10).

Moses asked Jethro his father-in-law to let him go and return to his brethren in Egypt. Jethro's answer was, "Go in peace" (Exod. 4:18).

Moses was eighty years of age when he stood before Pharaoh, and made the Lord God of Israel's request of him, "Let my people go." And Pharaoh said, "Who is the Lord, that I should obey his voice to let Israel go? I know not the Lord, neither will I let Israel go" (Exod. 5:1-2).

Moses was downcast in spirit when he returned unto the Lord, but God reassured him that He hadn't forgotten His covenant with Abraham, Isaac, and Jacob, which included the children of Israel. Their deliverance from Egypt unto national status was forthcoming.

Moses and Aaron stood before Pharaoh many times and made the same request. Pharaoh was forewarned of the plagues Egypt would suffer by the hand of the God of Israel if he refused. The grievous plagues God visited upon the land of Egypt, Pharaoh, and the Egyptians, are well known, and how they didn't fall upon the land of Goshen and the children of Israel. The miraculous wonders God wrought upon the Egyptians repeatedly hardened Pharaoh's heart the more, but built hope in the hearts of the children of Israel. God, by His mighty power, was making Himself known to all peoples.

It was after God sent thick darkness on the land of Egypt for three days (there was light in the dwellings of the children of Israel) that Pharaoh ordered Moses from him, to "see my face no more" (Exod.10:28), and further threatened him. "Moses said, 'Thou hast spoken well, I will see thy face again no more'" (Exod. 10:29). Pharaoh had literally sinned away his day of grace.

God instructed the congregation of Israel, through Moses and Aaron, on preparing the feast of the Passover, and on how the ordinance was to be observed. They were to strike the blood of the sacrificed lamb on the side posts and lintel of the door of each house, a token of family identity with the Lamb of God, the Redeemer, the promised One. They were to eat in haste and be prepared for their exodus from Egypt. That night God passed through the land of Egypt, smiting the firstborn of man and beast, but upon the sight of the blood, the token of Israel to Him, He passed over their homes and the plague was not upon them. "And this day shall be unto you for a memorial; and ye shall keep it a feast to the Lord throughout your generations; ye shall keep it a feast by an ordinance for ever" (Exod. 12:14).

God delivered the children of Israel from the Egyptians and led them, their flocks and their herds, through the way of the wilderness of the Red Sea. The Lord went before them by day in a pillar of cloud, and by night in a pillar of fire. Pharaoh was told of their flight. His heart and the hearts of his servants were hardened the more against God and His people. The Egyptians pursued them. When Pharaoh drew nigh, the children of Israel were sore afraid and cried unto God. After all they had witnessed of the mighty power of God, their faith in God was weak at best. God didn't let them seethe in their fear, but was merciful and provided a way of escape that they might bear the trials of liberation; they were oblivious to their addiction to servitude. When the Egyptians drew nigh, God, by a strong east wind, divided the waters of the Red Sea for the Israelites to pass through on dry land, but the walls of water collapsed on the Egyptians in pursuit. This was but the beginning of their three months' journey to Sinai.

They were a homeless and restless people as they traveled. They were discontent with their rations; were hungry to be back in Egypt, to sit by the flesh pots and eat their fill of bread. They chided and murmured against Moses and Aaron. They tempted the Lord, saying, "Is the Lord among us or not?" Moses repeatedly interceded for them. God was long-suffering and did many miraculous wonders to prove His presence: He sweetened the bitter water at Marah; rained manna from heaven for bread, caused quails to cover the ground for meat, brought forth water from the rock in Horeb when they thirsted, gave them victory when the Amaleks fought with them. This was all done over a relatively short period of time.

As they were nearing Sinai, Jethro, Moses' father-in-law, visited Moses. Moses greeted him warmly; did obeisance and kissed him. They asked each other of their welfare. "And Moses told his father-in-law all that the Lord had done unto Pharaoh and to the Egyptians for Israel's sake, and all the travail that had come upon them by the way, and how the Lord delivered them. And Jethro rejoiced for all the goodness which the Lord had done to Israel, whom he had delivered out of the hand of the Egyptians" (Exod. 18:8-9).

Jethro blessed God, and officiated a burnt offering in their worship together. It was revealing of the worthy respect Moses, Aaron, and the elders gave to Jethro, a gentile priest. The eating of bread together was further evidence of a kindred spirit in their bonds to God. Moses had been under the ministry of Jethro for forty years and was accustomed to him officiating the offerings, but to the others it was an acknowledgment of his high priestly calling of God.

On the morrow, Jethro took note of the tiring and time-consuming way Moses was judging his people. Moses listened to Jethro's wise counsel, which was of God, and readily followed it. He addressed both the administrative and judicial branches of government: how to make them effective in governing Israel. Jethro didn't tarry, but departed and went his way into his own land. Little is known of the personal life of Jethro, except of his worthiness. God entrusted him with Moses in the most critical years of his life, preparing him to be the leader of Israel.

Shortly after Jethro's visit, the children of Israel came to the desert of Sinai and camped at the base of Horeb, the mount of God. The journey had been trying for all of them. Their deliverance from Egypt didn't deliver them from their addiction to servitude. God's promises gave them hope and His wondrous works validated His promises, but were only priming to their faith. They were thinking in terms of the Old Covenant and had not been lifted to thinking in terms of a spiritual identity with God. Spiritual progress, however, was being made in their hearts.

Moses went up unto God, and, out of the mountain, the Lord called unto him. God proposed a covenant with the house of Jacob, and Moses was to speak these words of God to them: "Ye have seen what I did unto the Egyptians, and how I bare you on eagles' wings, and brought you unto myself. Now therefore, if ye will obey my voice indeed, and keep my covenant, then ye shall be a peculiar treasure unto me above all people: for all the earth is mine: and ye shall be unto me a kingdom of priests, and an holy nation" (Exod. 19:4-6).

Moses conferred with the elders and then laid the terms of the covenant before the people for ratification. "And all the people answered together, and said, 'All that the Lord hath spoken we will do.' And Moses returned the words of the people unto the Lord. And the Lord said unto Moses, 'Lo, I come unto thee in a thick cloud, that the people may hear when I speak with thee, and believe thee for ever.' And Moses told the words of the people unto the Lord" (Exod. 19:8-9). All in the camp trembled as they felt the presence of God and His awesome holiness. The Ten Commandments, written by the finger of God on tablets of stone and spoken by Moses to the people, are God's Standard of Righteousness written in the hearts of all peoples. They are like "directions for use" printed on the cover of any packaged product. They are in keeping with the way man was constituted to be in his relationship to God and to man, and, as precepts, would apply to all peoples. The terms of the covenant God made with Israel were essentially spiritual, but in a legal context. The Ten Commandments were inclusive in the terms of the covenant Israel was to keep, as were divers laws, ordinances, and rites of worship. The covenant was legal in character, and covered every phase of man's life: worship, domestic, and civic. All Israelites were subject to its terms whether they had a heart for God or not. They had no choice in the matter. The blessings of God for keeping covenant and the curses for breaking covenant were judgments visited upon Israel collectively—in current circumstances, transitory in character: blessings like favorable weather, bountiful crops, victories over their enemies, and the like, or curses like adversities, failure of crops, defeats in battles, and the like.

God was long-suffering. When a rebellious spirit pervaded the nation, timely warnings were given through prophets of God of impending judgments. Other nations witnessed both the blessings and the curses and were stricken with fear of the God of Israel. Israel was literally a national priesthood by the election of God, making God known to all peoples. Israel was a theocratic nation, governed by God.

God, in His covenant with Israel, was building on the promises He had made to Abraham, Isaac, and Jacob. The nation, Israel, is always in the historical context of God's revelation of Himself that culminated in Jesus Christ.

The moves made by Jacob and his family from Canaan to Egypt and then to Sinai were, in circumstances, providential and revealing of God, not only to Israel, but to all who hear and read of the miraculous wonders of God. He had but one objective—the revelation of Himself.

One can no more explain away the plagues of God on Egypt, and not on Goshen, by natural phenomenon, than the evolutionists can explain away the truth of the creationists.

At Sinai, Israel was being made ready for their wilderness journey to Canaan. "And let them make me a sanctuary; that I may dwell among them" (Exod. 25:8). Israel was to follow the pattern given by God in building the tabernacle: its furnishings, the outer court, its enclosures, the ark of the covenant and its rails and covering, and making it portable. Only that which gave grandeur befitting the glory of God was used and sanctified holy unto God.

God elected Aaron and his sons to minister the priest's office unto God. All that related to worship was by God's direction. The rites of worship were patterned after the worship given the Father by the only begotten Son of God in the spiritual manhood he had assumed in eternity—before time. Upon being elected by the Father to the office of the Great High Priest of all of fallen manhood, He gave Himself (the perfect man) as an offering (a living sacrifice) to the Father, on the behalf of and in identity with fallen manhood, to atone for the sins of the whole world: "on the behalf of" necessitates "identity with." An offering to God couldn't have been made in the place of another or in one's stead, simply because worship is personal. No one can take another's place in the worship of God.

The priests officiated all rites of worship. In offerings wherein blood was shed, the worshipper laid his hands on the head of the lamb to be sacrificed, prefiguring in type the offering of oneself in identity with the perfect One. One of many offerings, by the direction of God, would have acceptably expressed one's heart in his worship of God: the burnt offering or love offering, sin offering, peace offering, trespass offering, meat offering, to name the ones most common. All the offerings, in some way, prefigured in type that which would be fulfilled in Jesus Christ.

It was a very serious offense for one to break covenant. It brought a reproach upon Israel and was grounds for one being cut off from God. The offerings to restore covenant identity were by the direction of God and officiated by the priests. Atonements were made and the guilty forgiven. The restoration to covenant identity was not indicative of one's spiritual or personal status with God.

In a legal relationship, one has no choice but to comply with the terms. In a spiritual relationship, one can make choices. One can either have a responsive faith in God to do that which pleases Him, or one can do that which is self-serving. Motivation determines the difference.

Even though an Israelite's relationship to God, by covenant identity, was legal in character, he was also spiritually constituted to be personally related to God, as is all of manhood. His legal identity was academic to him in coming to know God in a personal way. One's knowledge of God is first academic before it becomes revelation. The number of Israelites would be countless, who, by the revelation God was giving of Himself, exercised the faith of Abraham.

Israel had been in Sinai for over two years. God didn't want them to sojourn there for long, but long enough to establish covenant identity which was centered in worship—man's only concourse to God. God, through Moses, spoke the rituals to be followed in the various offerings; addressed divers laws and ordinances. It was all of God. All of Israel was subject to the terms of the covenant, but the spirit in which they were executed could have been, objectively, personal or impersonal. Whether their hearts were in it or not, they would be blessed by God collectively as long as covenant was kept, but if it was broken, they would be cursed by God.

God was ready for them to be on the move again. They were yet forty years distant from crossing the Jordan into the promised land. God's protective care of Israel for the next several hundred years was nothing short of miraculous. The history of Israel in covenant identity with God took man's relationship to God out of the mystical into the real world.

Time was the essence of God's covenant with Israel: for its presentation and ratification; for the making of history in its execution; and for its termination. Covenant history allowed God to give a progressive unveiling of the revelation of Himself in circumstances with which man could and can relate. There was always a voice for God in the land. The prophets spoke the word of God and foretold future events. Credibility was built upon the coming to pass of what was foretold.

It isn't my intent to address the subject of prophecy, other than to cite a few references. Jacob was near death when he called together his sons to tell them what would befall them in the last days. His prophetic words to Judah distinguished him above his brothers. "Thou art he whom thy brethren shall praise" (Gen. 49:8). His most illustrious descendant was the incarnate Son of God, Jesus Christ, who, by direct reference, was the Lion of the tribe of Judah (Rev. 5:5). "The scepter shall not depart from Judah, nor a lawgiver from between his feet, until Shiloh come" (Gen. 49:10). These prophetic words were given long before there was a tribe of Judah.

The land of Canaan and some land on the east side of Jordan would be divided between the sons of Jacob into twelve tribal portions, but no less one nation, Israel. Levi was not given land, but was elected by God to the priesthood over all of Israel. The Levitical priesthood unified the nation in their worship of the only true and living God. The two sons of Joseph, Ephraim and Manasseh, were given portions, like a double inheritance to Joseph. Jacob's prophetic words to Joseph were as though they were already history, so truly did they come to pass.

Solomon sat upon the throne of David his father. Nearing the end of his reign, he saw that Jeroboam, his servant, was a mighty man of valor and industry. He made him ruler over all the charge of the house of Joseph. Jeroboam had discontent in his heart over Solomon's reign. Abijam, a prophet of God, found Jeroboam in a place where they were alone. He caught the new garment Jeroboam was wearing from off him and rent it in twelve pieces. "And he said to Jeroboam, 'take thee ten pieces: for thus saith the Lord, the God of Israel, "Behold, I will rend the kingdom out of the hand of Solomon, and will give ten tribes to thee: (But he shall have one tribe for my servant David's sake, the city which I have chosen out of all the tribes of Israel)" (1 Kings 11:31-32). The tribe of Judah was the chosen one, and Jerusalem was the city of David. Early in the reign of Rehoboam, Solomon's son, Abijam's prophecy came to pass. Israel was divided into two kingdoms: the northern and the southern.

David was of the tenth generation descended from Judah and was king over all of Israel. He carried the scepter of Judah proudly. His reign was not excelled prior to the coming of our Lord. Jesus was of the twenty-ninth generation descended from David. Jesus testified of Himself, "I am the root and the offspring of David, and the bright and morning star" (Rev. 22:16).

The Scriptures keep our Lord in close identity with Israel and the throne of David as history unveils the fulfilling of the promises of God made to Abraham, Isaac, and Jacob.

The wilderness journey from Sinai to Canaan was long, and tried the hearts of the children of Israel. But it also revealed the hand of God on their lives; and it revealed Himself to all nations.

After having passed Kadesh and Mount Hor, God gave the Israelites a solid victory over Sihon, the king of the Amorites, who had refused Israel's request to pass through the borders of his land—lying adjacent to the land of the Moabites. "And the children of Israel set forward, and pitched in the plains of Moab on this side of Jordan by Jericho. And Balak the son of Zippor [the king of Moab] saw all that Israel had done to the Amorites" (Num. 22:1-2).

Moab feared the Israelites, and, in a coalition with the Midianites, sent messengers, with the rewards of divination in their hands, to engage Balaam, a prophet of God, to curse Israel that they might prevail over them. They delivered the words of Balak, king of the Moabites, to Balaam, who sought enchantments from God against Israel, but was given only blessings. "And Balaam said to Balak, 'Behold, I have received commandment to bless: and he hath blessed; and I cannot reverse it. He hath not beheld iniquity in Jacob, neither hath he seen perverseness in Israel: the Lord his God is with him, and the shout of a king is among them. God brought them out of Egypt; he hath as it were the strength of an unicorn. Surely there is no enchantment against Jacob, neither is there any divination against Israel: according to this time it shall be said of Jacob and of Israel, 'What hath God wrought!'" (Num. 23:20-23).

Balak didn't give up, but sought a seance with Balaam a third time, but from another vantage point. The spirit of God came upon Balaam again, but with only blessings for Israel. "Blessed is he who blesseth thee and cursed is he that curseth thee" (Num. 24:9). Balak's anger was kindled against Balaam, who took up his parable again, and falling into a trance, but with his eyes open, prophesied what Israel would do to the Moabites in the latter days. "I shall see him, but not now: I shall behold him, but not nigh: there shall come a Star out of Jacob, and a Scepter shall rise out of Israel, and shall smite the corners of Moab, and destroy all the children of Sheth" (Num. 24:17).

Prophetic words that can be associated with the coming of our Lord are often quoted today. This is true of the words of Balaam which were spoken many hundreds of years before the birth of Jesus. God's protective care of Israel, as recorded in sacred history, is miraculous.

Balaam, the son of Beor, was known to the Moabites and Midianites as a prophet of God, and a diviner. Balak, the king of Moab in collusion with the Midianites, engaged his services to curse Israel on terms prearranged. The spirit of God came upon Balaam and gave him the words to speak. From the prophetic words he spoke, one could be led to think that he was a man of God. One usually associates the man with his message. It wasn't true in the case of Balaam. He was knowledgeable of the word of God; was given directions from God, but didn't have a place for God in his heart; lacked a love for God. His services were self-serving. Balaam had an untimely death. God ordered Moses to avenge the children of Israel on the Midianites. Israel warred against the Midianites, slew the five kings of Midian and also Balaam the son of Beor. (Num. 31) We learn from Peter, Jude, and John that he was a hireling prophet, loved the wages of unrighteousness, and was greedy for reward. It is sobering to think that one can mouth the words of God, yet be himself a castaway or reprobate. The Apostle Paul voiced this possibility (1 Cor. 9:27, and 2 Cor. 13:5).

The prophet, Micah, prophesied the birth of Jesus in Bethlehem some seven hundred years before it came to pass. "But thou, Bethlehem Ephratah, though thou be little among the thousands of Judah, yet out of thee shall he come forth unto me that is to be ruler in Israel; whose goings forth have been from of old, from everlasting" (Mic. 5:2).

In the days of Herod, the king of Judea, the history built on the promises of God to Abraham, Isaac, and Jacob was fast coming to fulfillment. An angel of the Lord appeared unto Zacharius, while serving at the altar of incense in the temple of the Lord, to tell him, "Thy prayer is heard; and thy wife Elisabeth shall bear thee a son, and thou shalt call his name John . . . He shall be called the prophet of the Highest and shall go before the face of the Lord to prepare His way" (Luke 1:13, 76). It came to pass as was foretold.

In the sixth month of Elisabeth's pregnancy, the angel, Gabriel, was sent from God to Mary, a virgin espoused to a man whose name was Joseph. The angel's salutation was, Hail, thou that art highly favored, the Lord is with thee: blessed art thou among women. "And the angel said unto her, 'Fear not, Mary: for thou hast found favour with God. And, behold, thou shalt conceive in thy womb, and bring forth a son, and shalt call his name JESUS. He shall be great, and shall be called the Son of the Highest: and the Lord God shall give unto him the throne of his father David: And he shall reign over the house of Jacob for ever; and of his kingdom there shall be no end'" (Luke 1:30-33). And Mary said, "Behold the handmaid of the Lord; be it unto me according to thy word. And the angel departed from her" (Luke 1:38). The angel of the Lord also appeared unto Joseph in a dream and allayed his fears, saying that Mary shall conceive by the Holy Ghost and bring forth a son, whom he shall call Jesus: for he shall save his people from their sins (Matt. 1:20-21).

At the decree from Caesar Augustus for all to be taxed, Joseph also went up from Galilee, out of the city of Nazareth, into Judea, to Bethlehem, the city of David (because he was of the house and lineage of David), to be taxed with Mary his espoused wife, who was great with child. Jesus was born in Bethlehem, as foretold by Micah.

Prophecy that had come to pass down through the years had given credibility to the prophets of the God of Israel. Upon hearing of the birth of the King of the Jews, Herod, the king, was troubled, along with all of Jerusalem. He gathered the chief priests and scribes of the people and demanded of them where Christ should be born. He then searched diligently, with what information he had, to find the child, not to worship Him, but to destroy Him. This is a surfacing of the warfare between the Serpent and the Seed of the woman.

"And when eight days were accomplished for the circumcising of the child, his name was called JESUS, which was so named of the angel before he was conceived in the womb. And when the days of her purification according to the law of Moses were accomplished, they brought him to Jerusalem, to present him to the Lord . . . And, behold, there was a man in Jerusalem, whose name was Simeon; and the same man was just and devout, waiting for the consolation of Israel: and the Holy Ghost was upon him. And it was revealed unto him by the Holy Ghost, that he should not see death, before he had seen the Lord's Christ. And he came by the Spirit into the temple: and when the parents brought in the child Jesus, to do for him after the custom of the law, then took he him up in his arms, and blessed God, and said, Lord, now lettest thou thy servant depart in peace, according to thy word: For mine eyes have seen thy salvation" (Luke 2:21-22, 25-30).

And there was a prophetess, Anna, "a widow of about fourscore and four years, which departed not from the temple, but served God with fastings and prayers night and day. And she coming in that instant gave thanks likewise unto the Lord, and spake of him to all them that looked for redemption in Jerusalem. And when they had performed all things according to the law of the Lord, they returned into Galilee, to their own city Nazareth. And the child grew, and waxed strong in spirit, filled with wisdom: and the grace of God was upon him" (Luke 2:37-40). My reader, think of what the testimony of Simeon and Anna must have meant to Mary and Joseph.

Knowledge of God is not innate in man, but, like all knowledge, is acquired. Man has an innate proclivity Godward and an aptitude to learn of God, but must be taught. What is academic becomes revelation to those who have hearts for God. A responsive love to God's love for one issues in a living bond to God that will find expression in word and deed.

Joseph and Mary were faithful in their stewardship in teaching the word of God to Jesus. His mind was not clouded by inherited depravity, but was clear to learn quickly. At the age of twelve, they found Him in the Temple, sitting in the midst of the doctors, both hearing them, and asking them questions. All that heard Him were astonished at His understanding and answers. He left the Temple, wholly submissive to His parents, and traveled back to Nazareth in company with them. "And Jesus increased in wisdom and stature, and in favour with God and man" (Luke 2:52). The Scriptures are then silent on the life of Jesus until He nears His thirtieth year.

Part V
The Fall and Redemption of Man

God's covenant with Abraham was by promise. Abraham believed God. His faith never wavered. He passed the crucial test of his faith by doing God's bidding, offering Isaac in sacrifice to Him. God said, "By myself have I sworn, saith the Lord, for because thou hast done this thing, and hast not withheld thy son, thine only son: That in blessing I will bless thee, and in multiplying I will multiply thy seed as the stars of the heaven, and as the sand which is upon the sea shore; and thy seed shall possess the gate of his enemies; And in thy seed shall all the nations of the earth be blessed; because thou hast obeyed my voice" (Gen. 22:16-18). "Now to Abraham and his seed were the promises made. He saith not, 'and to seeds,' as of many; but as of one, 'and to thy seed,' which is Christ" (Gal. 3:16). By the election of God, Abraham had the distinct honor of his posterity being the line of the Seed.

The genealogy of our Lord was recorded by both Matthew and Luke. It is of interest to note that Matthew, who was primarily writing to the Jew, carried the genealogy of our Lord back to Abraham, who was a Gentile, while Luke, who was primarily writing to the Gentiles, carried the genealogy of our Lord back to Adam.

From the time God made his promises to Abraham, the clock started objectively toward fulfilling them. The same promises were made to Isaac and to Jacob. Up to this time, it was a Gentile world inclusive of all nations. One chronologist, quoted by Adam Clark, estimated a period of 2168 years from Adam to Jacob. From the posterity of Abraham, God elected to bring into being the nation Israel, a theocratic nation, to be the custodian of the divine oracles; to be a protectorate of the line of the Seed, and a witness to all peoples.

Israel was literally God's people by covenant identity. Their relationship to God was like a window through which all peoples of the world could see, in legal terms, what was required of man in his relationship to God and man. It could be seen that worship acceptable to God was offered in identity with the Lamb of God.

Jesus was nearing the age of thirty when the word of God came unto John, the son of Zacharius, in the wilderness. "And he came into all the country about Jordan, preaching the baptism of repentance for the remission of sins; As it is written in the book of the words of Esaias the prophet, saying, the voice of one crying in the wilderness, Prepare ye the way of the Lord, make his paths straight . . . And all flesh shall see the salvation of God" (Luke 3:3-4, 6). Baptism is associated with one's identity, and, in context, with covenant identity. Repentance was a turning from breaking covenant and towards keeping covenant. The exercise of repentance, in context, is correlated to faith. The baptism of repentance was the avowing anew of each Israelite to covenant identity with God.

By reason of the legal character of the covenant, the baptism of repentance did not necessarily imply or express a change in one's heart for God. John's message was piercing the hearts of all Israel. They came forth by the multitudes to be baptized of him. Their responses could have been self-serving, fleeing the wrath to come. John called them a generation of vipers, and told them to bring forth fruits worthy of repentance. Having Abraham as their father was not to be equated with being a child of God through a personal faith in the Messiah, a faith motivated by a love for God.

The message of John was charged with personal conviction of the imminence of the coming of the Messiah, Jesus.

His introduction of Jesus used words familiar to all Israel. "Behold the Lamb of God, which taketh away the sin of the world" (John 1:29). It was an Israelite's identity with the Lamb of God that made his worship acceptable to God. Jesus was the Messiah, the Lamb of God, and the fulfillment of all that prefigured Him, in type, in the rituals of worship ordained by God and observed by Israel.

"Then cometh Jesus from Galilee to Jordan unto John, to be baptized of him. But John forbad him, saying, 'I have need to be baptized of thee, and comest thou to me?' And Jesus answering said unto him, 'Suffer it to be so now: for thus it becometh us to fulfill all righteousness.' [Righteousness in this context has reference to observing the ordinances.] Then he suffered him. And Jesus, when he was baptized, went up straightway out of the water: and, lo, the heavens were opened unto him, and he saw the Spirit of God descending like a dove, and lighting upon him: And lo a voice from heaven, saying, 'This is my beloved Son, in whom I am well pleased'" (Matt. 3:13-17). By His baptism, He was officially assuming His priestly stewardship to Israel. Straightforthly Jesus, being full of the Holy Ghost, was led by the Spirit into the wilderness to be tempted by the devil for forty days. On each proposal to self-glory, Jesus answered by quoting the Word of God. His faith was unshaken.

"And Jesus returned in the power of the Spirit into Galilee: and there went out a fame of Him through all the region round about. And he taught in their synagogues, being glorified of all. And he came to Nazareth, where he had been brought up: and, as his custom was, he went into the synagogue on the Sabbath day, and stood up for to read. And there was delivered unto him the book of the prophet Esaias. And when he had opened the book, he found the place where it was written, 'The Spirit of the Lord is upon me, because he hath anointed me to preach the gospel to the poor; he hath sent me to heal the brokenhearted, to preach deliverance to the captives, and recovering of sight to the blind, to set at liberty them that are bruised, To preach the acceptable year of the Lord.' And he closed the book, and he gave it again to the minister, and sat down. And the eyes of all them that were in the synagogue were fastened on him. And he began to say unto them, 'This day is this Scripture fulfilled in your ears.' And all bare him witness, and wondered at the gracious words which proceeded out of his mouth. And they said, 'Is not this Joseph's son?'" (Luke 4:14-22). Jesus, discerning their thoughts, said to them, "No prophet is accepted in his own country," and cited Scripture references concurring. When they heard, they were filled with wrath and thrust Him out of the city. He passed through them and went His way to a city in Galilee, and taught them on the Sabbath days. "They were astonished at His doctrine, for His word was with power" (Luke 4:32).

Most of my readers have knowledge of what is written in the four Gospels. The miracles Jesus did were by the enablement of the Father. They were not proof of His deity, but were His credentials for credibility. He was God, but God self-limited to the manhood He had assumed. Jesus wanted a hearing from Israel to lift all Israelites from the legal character of the Law to a revelation of the spiritual values the Law held. Jesus taught the spiritual character of the kingdom of God in His sermon on the Mount, and the nature of one's personal identity in the kingdom of God in His parables—making known the unknown through the medium of the well known.

"In the mouth of two or three witnesses shall every word be established" (2 Cor. 13:1). The voice from heaven said, "Thou art my beloved Son; in thee I am well pleased" (Luke 3:22). John, seeing Jesus coming unto him said, "Behold the Lamb of God" (John 1:29). Jesus was talking with the woman of Samaria. "The woman saith unto him, 'I know that Messias cometh, which is called Christ: when He is come, He will tell us all things.' Jesus saith unto her, 'I that speak unto thee am He'" (John 4:25-26). Jesus wanted all peoples to know that He was the Messiah.

Most of my readers are not knowledgeable of the fact that the personal sacrifice our Lord made of Himself to redeem fallen man was a living sacrifice inclusive of His whole humiliation. The personal sacrifice the Son made in assuming His spiritual manhood to redeem fallen man was addressed in chapter one. He self-limited His Divine nature to the confines of human nature, making Himself subject to the Father, as are all manhood. The sacrifice He made of Himself can only be matched by infinite love. His relationship to the Father in eternity, before time, was in the spiritual manhood He assumed. He was in a state of celestial glory, a foretaste of what His relationship to the Father would be in His glorified manhood. This glorious anticipation was in His thoughts when nearing His crucifixion: "And now, O Father, glorify thou me with thine own self with the glory which I had with thee before the world was" (John 17:5).

It was a further unveiling of His love: for His spiritual manhood to assume mortal manhood. That holy thing planted in the womb of the virgin Mary by the Holy Spirit was the mortal body being prepared for Jesus by the Father. (This subject is addressed at length in Appendix D.) "A body hast thou prepared me" (Heb. 10:5). He was made like unto His brethren, sin apart. The mortal man is subject to time; has his life cycle: a time to be born and a time to die. The mortal man is terminal at death, at which time, the spiritual man is released: the spiritual man never dies, but is eternal. One's birth, and death, can be untimely, but are the beginning and ending of one's life cycle—a lifetime experienced once. The offering of the body of Jesus Christ, once for all, was the lifetime sacrifice He made of Himself in the mortal manhood He assumed. The crucifixion of Jesus was a climax of faith and unbelief in contrast, and a prelude to resurrection, glory, and condemnation, respectively.

There is no place in the four Gospels where the crucifixion is associated with being the payment of a penal judgment for sin in the sinner's stead. Jesus had told His disciples, several times, in different ways, how He would be killed and raised the third day, but when it came to pass, at first they didn't remember. The words He had spoken were prophetic. "And now I have told you before it come to pass, that, when it is come to pass, ye might believe" (John 14:29). When the fulfillment of His words registered with them, it was timely, and bolstered their faith. In the Acts of the Apostles, where Luke writes of the missionary journeys of Paul, the crucifixion of Jesus was not associated with the payment of a penal judgment for sin in the sinner's stead.

The kind of death our Lord died in order to redeem fallen man was spiritual in character. He said, "I lay down my life for the sheep" (John 10:15). The verb "lay" is in the present tense. The present tense in the Greek, unless the context rules otherwise, has the force of continuity—I am continually laying down my life for the sheep. It couldn't have been a literal kind of death. The counterpart to our Lord's laying down His life for man is the laying down of man's life for Him, creating a living bond to God. The laying down of our Lord's life in the crucifixion was spiritual in character. It was the terminal part of His humiliation in the mortal manhood He assumed; the fulfilling of His stewardship in keeping with the will of the Father; and was the epitome of faith motivated by love.

To make the crucifixion of Jesus the payment of a penal judgment for sin in the sinner's stead is to make man's relationship to God legal or impersonal. But man's relationship to God is spiritual: personal in character. "God is a Spirit: and they that worship Him must worship Him in spirit and in truth" (John 4:24). As a result of sinning, one suffers a personal loss, spiritual in character, not a penal judgment, legal in character.

My reader would be better informed by reading the historical briefing of Israel given by Stephen, who called his Hebrew brethren betrayers and murderers of the Just One (Acts 7:52). The trial and conviction of our Lord for blasphemy was the greatest travesty of justice ever perpetrated. Mortal death was the most severe judgment the judiciary could impose. Mortal death, the crucifixion our Lord suffered, terminated His life cycle, but had no effect on the spiritual kind of death our Lord was experiencing in redeeming fallen man. It was never terminal, but was inclusive of His whole humiliation in eternity, before time, in time, and after time. He will always be God, self-limited to the confines of the human nature He assumed. In eternity, in the ages to come, the Father will show "the exceeding riches of His grace in His kindness toward us through Christ Jesus" (Eph. 2:7).

"Eye hath not seen, nor ear heard, neither have entered into the heart of man, the things which God hath prepared for them that love him" (1 Cor. 2:9). "For the kingdom of God is not meat and drink; but righteousness, and peace, and joy in the Holy Ghost" (Rom. 14:17). The kingdom of God is spiritual in character. "Now this I say, brethren, that flesh and blood cannot inherit the kingdom of God; neither doth corruption inherit incorruption" (1 Cor. 15:50). God created man bipartite, body and spirit. The body houses the spirit in time, and is mortal, subject to death. This mortal must put on immortality. Our Lord is our file leader. At His resurrection, His mortal put on immortality, His glorified body. All believers have this hope. The whole man, body and spirit will be redeemed, the spirit in this lifetime and the body in eternity. In eternity our Lord alone has immortality (1 Tim. 6:16).

It is reasonable to think that the redeemed in eternity are clothed upon, and are awaiting their glorified bodies. Those in time and in eternity are anticipating the consummation of their redemption, to wit, the unifying hope of their glorified bodies. (Rom. 8: 19-25)

In a lifetime, one is saved or lost as he relates to a living bond to God. In either case, one will suffer a personal loss as a consequence of his sin. There will be degrees of celestial glory for the saved and, conversely, degrees of damnation for the lost. One's lifetime is probationary to eternity, and lived out in one's mortal body. The determining factor of one's eternal state is one's relationship to Jesus Christ in time. The Apostle Paul admonishes the Ephesians to walk "not as fools, but as wise, redeeming the time, because the days are evil" (Eph. 5:15-16).

The personal losses, suffered as a consequence of sin, accumulate in one's spiritual stature. One is continually picking up his wages of sin. Sin dwarfs one's heart for God. God is being crowded out of one's life. One will bask in the sun of God's mercies without serious thought of God. When God is not a part of one's life in time, how can one relate to a living bond to God in eternity? When mortal death comes to the unbeliever, he is lost to the benefits from God enjoyed in time, and finds himself in utter darkness without God, without the benefits from God, but still with the appetites of the natural man, with no way to satisfy them. How could hell or damnation be more vividly described? The account of the rich man and Lazarus tells it realistically (Luke 16:20-31).

There is anticipation of celestial glory in the hearts of all believers. All will be rewarded in keeping with the earnestness of their hearts for God in time. The Apostle Paul expressed it in this way, "I press toward the mark for the prize of the high calling of God in Christ Jesus" (Phil. 3:14). Moses "esteemed the reproach of Christ greater riches than the treasures in Egypt: for he had respect unto the recompense of the reward (Heb. 11:24-28). "And whatsoever ye do, do it heartily, as to the Lord, and not unto men; knowing that of the Lord ye shall receive the reward of the inheritance, for ye serve the Lord Christ" (Col. 3:23-24). "For whatsoever a man soweth, that shall he also reap" (Gal. 6:7). The Apostle Paul speaks of the degrees of celestial glory: "For one star differeth from another star in glory. So also is the resurrection of the dead" (1 Cor. 15:41-42). All of the above would be without meaning if something special was not in store in eternity, for the faithful in time.

It is the revelation of God's love for one that is most effectual in drawing one to God. What greater message of God's love could there be than that of God wanting to share His life with one? The believer's response of faith to the Gospel is like a romance that culminates in a marriage to the Son of God. All believers collectively become the bride of Jesus Christ, members of the family of God for all eternity.

God's love for man has no time factor: it is the same in time as it is in eternity. God's love acts spontaneously in His care for man. It is instinctively known to all, and is discerned in providential circumstances by those whose hearts are attuned to God. The love innate in man's image of God is instinctively exemplified in a mother's love. One's response to God's love for him and man's caring love for others is indicative of his spiritual state.

The fall of Adam and Eve and their response to God's redeeming love were addressed in Chapter One. They believed God; put their trust in the Seed of the woman; and were the first to be born into the kingdom of God.

God is building His kingdom, in time, on the foundation of the Apostles and prophets, Jesus Christ Himself being the chief cornerstone. All believers and those who die in their innocence are living stones, fitly framed together, growing unto a holy temple in the Lord, for a habitation of God through the Spirit. Throughout time and in circumstances, the spirits of all manhood are tested. Redemption gives life to all who are reconciled to God through faith in Jesus Christ, and to all who are judged innocent by God.

The more one knows of God's love for oneself, the more God is endeared to one's heart. An appreciation of God's love is directly related to the revelation one has of God's love. It excites one's innate proclivity Godward and one's instinctive consciousness of being incomplete apart from God. One's responsive love to God's love creates a living bond to God, God's objective in redeeming fallen man. Our Lord's whole humiliation is an example of love. "God is love." When, in eternity, the Father gave His only begotten Son, and the Son gave of Himself to assume His spiritual manhood, they suffered infinite consequences to which the finite mind cannot relate. It affected their personal relationship on the Divine level. The Father's relationship to His Son in the manhood He assumed was on the level of human nature—the Son having self-limited His Divine nature to the confines of manhood.

The Son of God experienced a glorious relationship with the Father in the spiritual manhood He assumed in eternity. He was incomplete apart from His body, as man was created body and spirit. The mortal body houses the spiritual man in time. The Son was also incomplete apart from His complement, as Adam was without Eve. God sent His Son into the world to assume His mortal body and to gather together the redeemed, collectively, His bride.

The common objective of the Father and the Son was to redeem fallen man from a spiritual kind of death unto a spiritual kind of life as man relates to God. Redemption is spiritual in character. The message of redemption addresses each one personally.

If redemption was legal in character, it could be conferred on one like a degree of letters, and it could also be conferred collectively. Legal terms do not hold spiritual promises. Israel was never promised eternal life, individually or collectively, for keeping covenant.

Jesus came unto His own people, Israel, who were His by covenant identity. He was the fulfillment of all that prefigured Him, in type, in the rituals of worship Israel observed, and all that was prophesied of Him that had come to pass. The miracles He did gave Him credibility and a hearing.

Our Lord's message to Israel invited a personal response, but Israel's thoughts were in keeping with their national identity with God. The coming of the Messiah was their hope of redemption from subjugation to Rome to the restoration of the kingdom of God to Israel, a theocratic kingdom.

Israelites were accustomed to think in terms of covenant identity: blessings for keeping covenant and curses for breaking covenant. For all who were personally given to God, it would have been a way of life.

A large number of those of Christian persuasion today think in legal terms in their relationship to God, and are unaware that they are following the pattern of Israel under the Old Covenant. One is taught that God punishes sin, another that God is too merciful to punish sin. Both teachings proceed from the same legal premise and do not know it. It isn't easy for one who thinks from a legal premise to change his thought pattern. For example: the words of Micah, a prophet of God in the days of Ahaz and Hezekiah, kings of Judah, are often lifted from their legal context to serve a spiritual end, and one may not know the difference. "Wherewith shall I come before the Lord, and bow myself before the high God? He hath shewed thee, O man, what is good; and what doth the Lord require of thee, but to do justly, and to love mercy, and to walk humbly with thy God?" (Mic. 6:6-8). One might ask, "What more can one do than what is required of him?" The answer is, "Nothing," but it doesn't make for a personal or spiritual bond to God. The steward of a household may do all that is required of him, but it doesn't make him one of the family. Man's relationship to God is spiritual or personal in character, not legal or impersonal.

Legal actions or overtures are self-serving, expecting something in return for what is given, whether in services or in pay of some kind.

Spiritual actions or overtures, when motivated by love, are the giving of oneself to enrich another without thought of receiving something in return. A living bond is being nurtured. It was hard for Israel to think in terms of the spiritual, of God's love for them and His wanting to share His life with them. After the feeding of the five thousand, a number believed He was the Messiah, and would have made Him king over Israel, but not king over their own hearts.

Jesus likened Himself to living water, a well of water springing up unto everlasting life, and to bread which comes down from heaven and gives life to the world: "He that eateth my flesh, and drinketh my blood, dwelleth in me, and I in him. As the living Father hath sent me, and I live by the Father: so he that eateth me, even he shall live by me" (John 6:56-57). Jesus, knowing that they murmured among themselves, said to them, "Doth this offend you?" (John 6:61). Then He explained further: "It is the spirit that quickeneth; the flesh profiteth nothing: the words that I speak unto you, they are spirit, and they are life" (John 6:63).

This life Jesus imparts is actually a spiritual quickening by the Spirit of Jesus in the believer. "But ye are not in the flesh, but in the Spirit, if so be that the Spirit of God dwell in you. Now if any man have not the Spirit of Christ, he is none of His" (Rom. 8:9). Eternal life is a living bond to Jesus and will be lived in the spirit of worship, making manifest God's love for one and one's love for God. "And whatsoever ye do in word or deed, do all in the name of the Lord Jesus, giving thanks to God and the Father by him" (Col. 3:17).

One who lives in the spirit of worship will have the constraint of God's love to keep oneself in the way everlasting. It is like marital bonds that have the blessing of God. They are lived in the spirit of devotion to each other. All that either one does, even unconsciously, has the constraint of the other's love. How could love be expressed any better than for one to want to share one's life with another? Jesus wanted His life, in word and deed, to be revelation of who He was to all of Israel, enlisting a personal response.

"And John calling unto him two of his disciples sent them to Jesus, saying, 'Art thou he that should come, or look we for another?' . . . Then Jesus answering said unto them, 'Go your way, and tell John what things ye have seen and heard; how that the blind see, the lame walk, the lepers are cleansed, the deaf hear, the dead are raised, to the poor the gospel is preached" (Luke 7:19,22). This was prophesied of the Messiah by Isaiah. John got the message. The Jews, round about Jesus in the temple, in Solomon's porch, said to Him, "How long dost thou make us to doubt? If thou be the Christ, tell us plainly." [Either they didn't know or were blinded to what was prophetic of Jesus in the Scriptures.] Jesus answered them, "The works that I do in my Father's name, they bear witness of me" (John 10:24-25). The Pharisees and the chief priests sent officers to take Jesus. When they returned without Him, they were asked, "'Why have ye not brought Him?' The officers answered, 'Never man spake like this man'" (John 7:45-46).

Jesus wanted His works and His words to be revelation to them of who He was: the Messiah, the Redeemer, the lover of their souls. To have been told by Him who He was, apart from it being revelation to them, would have been like having the answer and not knowing the subject. When one senses a caring for oneself by another, it bears a spiritual message that has an inexplainable drawing power. Love begets love. Love is a quality of being that reaches out to give of oneself for another. It is spontaneous action that stems from one's heart without thought for oneself.

One comes to know God through a progressive unveiling of the historical revelation God is giving of Himself. As one is responsive to the light one has, more light will be given. There is always the possibility of being too defensive of what one has been taught and thus not allowing one's thinking to be challenged. My own writings are a good example of changes in my thinking as a further unveiling of God's revelation comes to me. One ought not to feel offended when one's thinking is challenged; possibly there is good reason to give the subject more thought (have Berean zeal, Acts 17:11). The Apostle Paul said to Timothy, "Consider what I say; and the Lord give thee understanding in all things" (2 Tim. 2:7).

"For God sent not his Son into the world to condemn the world; but that the world through him might be saved. He that believeth on him is not condemned: but he that believeth not is condemned already, because he hath not believed in the name of the only begotten Son of God (John 3:17-18). God's objective in sending His Son into the world was spiritual in character, to redeem man from a spiritual kind of death as he relates to God unto a spiritual kind of life. One who believes is responsive to God's love; is born into a living bond to God. One who does not believe is already in a spiritual state of death as one relates to God, not having responded to God's love and not having believed in the name of the only begotten Son of God. Believing is an exercise of faith.

Faith is a faculty, like the faculty of sight. It is a gift everyone has from God. The exercise of faith is personal in character. It can be objectively impersonal, like having faith in the operation of your car, or in having faith in God that is self-serving, for what He can do or has done for you, or believing in God for whatever one's imagination affords. In faith that is self-serving, there is not likely to be any personal interaction with God.

Our Lord assumed mortal manhood in circumstances with which man can relate. He was made like unto His brethren, sin apart. His knowledge of God was not innate, but acquired. His eagerness to learn of God was like that of any child. Joseph and Mary were faithful stewards in teaching Him from the Scriptures, and in giving Him parental love and guidance.

One is most apt to engage in dialogue on a subject that holds one's interest. The conference Jesus had with the doctors in the Temple at twelve years of age tells us wherein His mind trafficked. He was hearing them and asking them questions. There is nothing more stimulating to one's thinking than in having dialogue. The logic of one's reasoning is open to challenge. There can be very little interest in a subject in which one has no questions.

Our Lord grew in wisdom and in stature, and in favor with God and man (paraphrase of Luke 2:52). For Him to have been the reader of the Scriptures in the synagogue on the Sabbath day was an acknowledgment of His qualification. He was familiar to those in his home town: "Is not this Joseph's son?" (Luke 4:22) gives us something of His profile in the minds of them who knew Him, and tells us that they knew nothing phenomenal about His life. His walk and communion with the Father were personal, and made manifest in an orderly life. His time had not yet come. Following His baptism by John, the Spirit of the Lord was upon Him. He had the anointing of God to assume His priestly ministry to Israel.

The multitudes heard Him gladly. The religious establishment, fostered by the Pharisees, opposed Him. They were vocal and accused Him falsely. He looked down over Jerusalem and wept. His own people had rejected Him. He had the company of His disciples and the warmth of family love from Mary, Martha, and Lazarus. His strength came from His communion with the Father.

Jesus was faithful in His mission to redeem man. He was the justifier of manhood in that He was man in a living bond to the Father, as God created man to be. He was to the glory of the Father and was revelation to man, wherein man will find fulfillment in God's objective for man. "He that hath the Son hath life, he that hath not the Son of God hath not life" (1 John 5:12).

God is reconciled to man by the faith of Jesus. The Gospel bids man to be reconciled to God by faith in Jesus, faith motivated by love for God. The life the Father gave unto His Son, in the manhood He assumed, is given or channeled to all believers. All believers are in a marital bond to Jesus and make up the family of God. All believers are adopted sons of God and joint heirs with the Son of God to all the riches the kingdom of God holds.

It is logical and reasonable that there will be no judiciary in heaven as it is known to us in time. Where there is no sin there is no administration of law. There will be the final judgment, wherein our Lord officiates. This judgment will be an affirmation of what has already taken place in time as touching the culmination of one's spiritual stature. He calls it as he knows it to be, and His judgment is just (John 5:30). It will be in keeping with the preeminence God has been given in one's heart in time, and of one's faithfulness in stewardship. These are determining factors in qualifying one for his place in the family of God in eternity, and for the celestial glory that will be his. The sacrifices stemming from one's heart, motivated by a love for God, will never go unrewarded.

All believers anticipate a glorious life in the family of God in eternity, wherein love for God and for each other reigns in every heart. With the judgment of God behind them, all would have been awarded their degree of celestial glory. There will probably be tears of joy and regrets. The Apostle John gives us this comfort: the Lamb which is in the midst of the throne shall wipe away all tears, clearing our eyes to behold the wonders of His grace and lifting us above all regrets to a life of happiness forevermore (Rev. 7:17).

Summary

The following summarizes the logical conclusion of the sacrifices made by the Father and the Son in eternity, in time, and back in eternity with all the redeemed.

The personal sacrifices made by the Father and His only begotten Son in eternity to redeem fallen man didn't affect the Divine nature of the Son, or His Sonship to the Father, which were by eternal generation. It affected the relationship they had in the Divine family wherein kinship and endearment for each other found expression on the Divine level. In laying down their lives for man, a new relationship was created—that of the Father with the Son in the manhood He had assumed. Their former relationship would never be the same again. In explanation: by natural generation my son's nature will always be human nature and his sonship will never change. However, his relationship to me would change when he assumed married life. He would leave what had been home to him to establish a home of his own—another family entity. Later, my son returns home bringing his family with him. Our joys are multiplied. I feel deeply honored in having my son, my grandson, and my great grandson bearing my full name: in my lifetime, four generations of being kindred in a family bond. One who lays down one's life for another never lays down as much as one picks up. One picks up the abundant life. This is a principle: a fundamental rule that applies to all, even to God.

Subjectively, the personal cost to one of that which is done for another, when motivated by love, isn't reckoned in terms of sacrifice. It is done spontaneously according to the need.

The Son of God, in the spiritual manhood He assumed, was incomplete apart from a body. God created man body and spirit. He was also incomplete apart from His bride, as Adam was incomplete apart from Eve. He left His Father's house in eternity to assume His mortal body prepared for Him by the Father; to further seek out His bride in time; to fulfill the promises made before His first coming; and to add more believers to the sharing of His life in time. All believers are in a marital bond to the Son of God, they bring praise and glory to the Father, literally building the family of God, the kingdom of God. The delights of the Father are multiplied by the millions endeared to His heart by their responsive love to His love for them. The Son ends His mission in time and returns to His Father's house in eternity while still adding believers to His family; by the regenerating power of the Holy Spirit, all believers are children of God by adoption. There is only one only begotten Son of God. At the consummation of time the whole body of believers will be His bride and in eternity will feast together at the marriage supper of the Lamb. The Son, in His glorified manhood, will sit on the throne of God at the right hand of His Father, assuming headship over His family, to the exaltation of the Father and to the glorious joy of all the redeemed.

A Review

The Bible is a progressive unveiling of God's historical revelation of Himself that culminated in Jesus Christ. One can miss so much by not knowing the continuity of the message it bears. It is hoped that this book will be helpful in filling in some of what has been missed. One's faith can be no greater than the revelation one has of God.

The delights of God the Father and His only begotten Son were in the sons of men before time. The creation of the world of nature was with man in mind and would have been without meaning apart from man. What greater love could one have than to want to share his life with another? God's objective in creating man was to share His life with man. God's first thoughts after creation were on being in communion with man. Adam and Eve, in their flawless state, would have quickly responded to a communiqué from God, a spiritual phenomenon dulled in man's depraved nature, but known in measure to all of fallen man.

Adam and Eve lived in the spirit of worship as they related to God, and in the spirit of devotion as they related to each other. The utopia in which they lived had the spiritual climate of God's sunshine and the warmth of God's love. All of natural creation carried a message of God's love to them as it does to man today. Don't miss it.

The sacred history of the life God was sharing with Adam and Eve in the garden of Eden is brief, probably because fallen man cannot relate to man's relationship to God in a flawless state. Man is a created personality; has latitude to express free agency; was created peccable, vulnerable to temptation. God doesn't tempt man. Adam and Eve were lured by the subtlety of God's arch enemy, Satan, to sin. Consequently, they suffered a spiritual kind of death, as they related to God, and a depraved nature.

The revelation of God's love for man finds expression to the uttermost in the redemption of fallen man from a spiritual kind of death unto a spiritual kind of life as one relates to God. The personal sacrifices made by God the Father and His only begotten Son to redeem fallen man are beyond what the finite mind can relate: God the Father gave His only begotten Son, never to have Him back again on the Divine level, but on the level of human nature. The only begotten Son of God gave of Himself to the human nature He assumed, self-limiting His Divine nature to the confines of human nature, making Himself subject to the Father as is all of manhood.

The theme of the Bible is redemption. The message of the Bible is how it is made effectual in the hearts of men. This book addresses the subject of redemption from a spiritual premise. Man's relationship to God is spiritual in character, not legal.

All of manhood were in the loins of Adam when Adam sinned. Consequently, his posterity suffers the same kind of death, and a depraved nature, as Adam suffered. All of fallen manhood are spiritually and genetically related to their progenitors: "the iniquity of the fathers is visited upon their children unto the third and fourth generation" (Num. 14:18). Only that which is spiritual or biological is transmitted genetically, like spiritual traits, temperament, the characteristics of a depraved nature, and possibly contagious diseases. That which is legal in character, like a penal judgment, cannot be transmitted through the genes. Redemption, being spiritual in character, does not address legal judgments.

In man's depravity, the best he can do comes short of the glory of God. All of the faculties of the depraved man are functionally impaired in some way. Man is as prone to sin as sparks fly upward: "All sins shall be forgiven unto the sons of men" (Mark 3:28). The unpardonable sin is the sin of unbelief. When man's heart reaches a state of unbelief, he is in a state of condemnation. Only God knows man's spiritual state. Our Lord said unto the woman taken in adultery, "'Hath no man condemned thee?' She said, 'No man, Lord.' And Jesus said unto her, 'Neither do I condemn thee: go, and sin no more'" (John 8:10-11). Condemnation is consequential to unbelief in Jesus. "For God sent not his Son into the world to condemn the world; but that the world through him might be saved" (John 3:17). Forgiveness does not negate the consequence of sin nor license one to continue in sin. Man will suffer the consequences of his sin, affecting his spiritual stature, the kind of person he is becoming, but will not suffer a legal judgment.

In redemption, God addresses man's spiritual state. God lifts fallen man by revealing His love for him; not by first putting him down, like faulting a cripple because he has fallen, but by lifting him from a crippled state to being made whole, complete in a living bond to God through faith in Jesus Christ, faith motivated by a love responsive to God's love.

Following the confession of Adam and Eve's faith in the Seed of the woman, God ordained rituals of worship for them and all successive generations to observe until what was prefigured in type was fulfilled in Jesus Christ. The rituals, like the message they carried, never changed. They were to them like the message of the Bible is to us. The Holy Spirit takes the message of God and makes it revelation to all who have responsive hearts.

Abel got the message, as did Seth, Noah, Abraham, Isaac, Jacob, Joseph, Moses, and Jethro the priest of Midian. They were the principals in sacred history before Sinai and the ratifying of the Old Covenant by the children of Israel.

It was a Gentile world for some twenty-five hundred years before God brought into being the nation Israel, a theocratic nation, (a nation ruled by God), from the seed of Abraham. By the promises of God, Abraham not only fostered a nation, but became the progenitor of the line of the Seed in which Abraham's faith rested by promise. The promises of God were also made to Isaac and Jacob. God became known to successive generations as the God of Abraham, Isaac, and Jacob.

This book relates the history of a nation in the making, of the birth of the nation, Israel, from Abraham's seed. The children of Israel were delivered from Egyptian captivity by the hand of God. They became a national entity which has never been lost to this day.

Israel was a theocratic nation bonded to the true and living God by covenant identity. She harbored the Seed of the woman until the promises of God, prefigured in type in the rituals of worship, were fulfilled in Jesus Christ.

At Sinai, at the base of Mt. Horeb, the children of Israel ratified the covenant proposed by God and mediated by Moses. God's hand on Israel for the next several hundred years is a large part of sacred history. The faithfulness of God in keeping covenant with Israel enlightened the Gentile world. Promises made and prophecy foretold, being fulfilled, gave credibility to the word of God and to the prophets of God. Sacred history as it becomes known today makes for revering God as it did in the days it was being made.

Israel is the only theocratic nation known to man. Unlike an autocracy, latitude was given to express free agency. Israel was subject to a standard of righteousness, whose author was God. Israel was to give God the preeminence in religious, domestic, and civic life: all three were addressed in the terms of the Old Covenant. Israel, by covenant identity, was in a legal relationship to God single to her. All Israelites were subject to the terms of the covenant. Compliance to that which was essentially spiritual in character was legally exacted. The disposition of depraved man caused many Israelites to revolt inwardly against threats for breaking covenant. The spirit that pervaded the nation made for blessings or curses from God. An Israelite in an impersonal way was legally related to God, but spiritually related to God in a personal way. Keeping covenant could be impersonal in character and did not necessarily imply a personal response to God's love.

God divided the nation Israel into twelve tribes after the twelve sons of Jacob, and also the land of Canaan into twelve portions. This was in the latter days of Reoboam, Solomon's son, and king over Israel. Joseph was given two portions, which he divided between his two sons, Ephraim and Manasseh. Levi was not given a portion of land, but was elected by God to the priesthood over all the tribes of Israel. The nation was unified in a spiritual bond that distinguishes it from other peoples to this day. Israel is a living monument of its sacred history. Their witness for God still lives in their emeritus state. The Jew has never lost his national identity. The nation Israel, in territory, is about the size of the state of Vermont; is associated with world powers; and is kept afloat by the providence of God. It is nothing short of miraculous; makes manifest a work of God; and can be witnessed by the people of all nations.

Israel's era of covenant identity with God came to a close shortly after the coming of Jesus and His priestly ministry to Israel. The Old Covenant, which was legal in character, was supplanted by the New Covenant, which is spiritual in character. At Pentecost, God expanded the priesthood of His appointment to a body of priests, with Jesus Christ our high priest.

The prophetic words of Micah, after a lapse of seven hundred years, came to pass as predicted. Jesus was born in Bethlehem in Judea. God the Father sent His only begotten Son into the world to assume His mortal body: "a body hast thou prepared me" (Heb. 10:5). He was made like unto His brethren, sin apart. He came in person to fulfill what was prefigured of Him in type in the rituals of worship, and to seek out His bride: those who believed in Him before and after His coming. All believers collectively are the bride of Jesus. The woman of Samaria said, "'when He is come, He will tell us all things.' Jesus saith unto her, 'I that speak unto thee am he'" (John 4:25-26).

The early ministry of our Lord is addressed briefly in this book. Jesus was introduced to Israel by John the Baptist in words directly relating to temple worship. The words of John, "Behold the Lamb of God" (John 1:36), heralded Jesus to be the fulfillment in person of what prefigured Him in type in the rituals of worship ordained by God and observed by Israel.

All Israelites were programmed in the worship of God from their youth and were taught the ceremonial rites of worship to be observed. Threats of judgment gave them an awesome fear of God. The worship of God officiated by the Levitical priesthood was central to the life of Israel and kept their covenant identity with God the priority of their lives. The rites of worship and the atonements for sin (love offerings and sin offerings) found expression by offering appropriate sacrifices in following the rites of worship they had been taught. An Israelite would bring a sin offering, a living sacrifice, to the altar of worship, to be officiated by a priest. He would lay his hands on the head of the lamb to be offered, signifying identity with the promised One in type. His offering was acceptable to God, an atonement made, his sins forgiven, and his covenant identity back on track. I want my reader to see that covenant identity with God gave Israel collectively an umbrella coverage of God's protective care, apart from one's personal relationship to God. What was required of one legally would not necessarily have enlisted a personal response to God's love for him. The terms of the old covenant were legal in character, but essentially spiritual in essence. Had they not been, they wouldn't have carried a personal message. Many in Israel got the message. Three thousand came forward at Pentecost.

The message of Jesus to Israel ministered to the inner man; gave hope; fed spiritual hunger, a hunger everybody has. The multitudes pressed to hear Him. His words on the kingdom of God were spoken in parables in circumstances with which they could relate. It made them want to be a part of the kingdom He was talking about. While He was enlisting their faith in Him, to be personally included in the kingdom of God, they were thinking of collective identity, not personal identity. Their hope rested in the Messiah restoring the kingdom of God to Israel, and delivering them from subjugation to Rome. When one's thoughts of God rest on a legal premise, it will tend to make one's response self-serving and unmindful of Him.

It doesn't come easy for one who has been taught redemption from a legal premise to think on the subject from a spiritual premise. My reader can readily see how true this was with Israel in her day, but it is no less true today with those who hold that God sent His only begotten Son into the world on a legal mission.

The whole humiliation of our Lord epitomizes the laying down His life for man, which is synonymous to expressing one's love for another. Jesus said, "Greater love hath no man than this, that a man lay down his life for his friends" (John 15:13). He is the "Lamb slain from the foundation of the world" (Rev. 13:8). From the foundation of the world is without termination. "And he is the propitiation for our sins: and not for ours only, but also for the sins of the whole world" (1 John 2:2). He is ever a propitiation for the sins of the whole world; an acceptable offering to the Father. Man has a ready access to the Father through Him. In the Greek, the present tense has the force of continuity. The sacrifice the only begotten Son of God made of Himself to redeem fallen man is spiritual in character; all-inclusive of the laying down His life in His spiritual manhood in eternity, His mortal manhood in time, and His immortal and glorified manhood in eternity. He anticipated His glorified state in company with all the redeemed, collectively His bride. Redemption, being spiritual in character, could not have been accomplished by legal means, not by the crucifixion, a single event in time.

The laying down of one's life has many synonyms in the Scriptures, finds expression in many ways: in the dying to one's self life, a spiritual kind of dying, the Apostle Paul said, "I die daily" (1 Cor. 15:31), and again, "That I may know him, and the power of his resurrection, and the fellowship of his sufferings, being made conformable unto his death" (Phil. 3:10). In this context, it couldn't have had reference to the crucifixion of our Lord. To paraphrase Rom. 6:5, "Except we be in the likeness of His death, we cannot be in the likeness of His resurrection." Our Lord said to His disciples, "If any man will come after me, let him deny himself, and take up his cross daily, and follow me" (Luke 9:23). There are three kinds of death contrasted in the Scriptures: mortal death, the termination of one's life cycle; the death that is experienced in unbelief and exclusion of God in one's life; and the death that is experienced in faith, motivated by a love for God.

The bearing of one's cross is spiritual or personal in character, whatever the circumstance. It sounds like a paradox, that life comes through a spiritual kind of death: the laying down of one's life for another. "Verily, verily, I say unto you, except a corn of wheat fall into the ground and die, it abideth alone: but if it die, it bringeth forth much fruit" (John 12:24). The personal enrichment consequential to the laying down of one's life for another, that one picks up more than he lays down, is a spiritual phenomenon that is unexplainable. One picks up the abundant life.

In our Lord's mortal manhood, He suffered many things at the hands of the Pharisees: mockery, contempt, conspiracy, and rejection. They were the leadership of the religious establishment of the day and the dominating influence in Israel's rejection of Jesus. Jesus, in compassion, looked over Jerusalem with a grief stricken heart and wept. His own people, in their delusion, had rejected Him. The council of the Pharisees instigated the greatest travesty of justice ever perpetrated, falsely accusing Jesus of blasphemy in a trial and conviction that led to His crucifixion.

In Gethsemane, after having eaten the Passover supper with His disciples, Jesus said unto them, "My soul is exceeding sorrowful unto death" (Mark 14:34). He prayed to the Father, "If it be possible, let this cup pass from me: nevertheless not as I will, but as thou wilt" (Matt. 26:39) His plea to the Father was made with a troubled spirit, "He went away again the second time, and prayed, saying, 'O my Father, if this cup may not pass away from me, except I drink it, thy will be done'" (Matt. 26:42). The will of God is spiritual in character and addresses one's person and one's office; one's person in keeping with the character of God and one's office in keeping with one's stewardship. The responses to the will of God are personal in character and find expression in obedience or disobedience. Motivation determines which. Circumstances are not to be equated with the will of God. It isn't the circumstance one faces, but the way one faces the circumstance that answers to the will of God. We can all relate to roadblocks, and hurdles to clear in the course of our lives. God has promised to give the enablement to meet them that we might bear them (1 Cor. 10:13). Jesus fulfilled His stewardship in yielding to the will of the Father as He had throughout His humiliation, in laying down His life to redeem fallen man from a spiritual kind of death, unto a spiritual kind of life.

In facing the crucifixion, the thoughts of Jesus were not on the pain He would suffer in His mortal body, His nail-pierced hands, the spear thrust into His side, and the crown of thorns He would wear. He was already suffering the sorrow of the inner man: being rejected by His own people, mocked, and the claims made of Himself discredited. The shame, degradation, and disdain in being crucified a malefactor and an evildoer would bring a reproach upon His Father. The laying down His life to redeem fallen man was spiritual in character, not legal; and evidenced in obedience.

"Who for the joy that was set before Him endured the cross, despising the shame, and is set down at the right hand of the throne of God" (Heb. 12:2). That one will pick up more than he lays down, when motivated by love, is an unexplainable spiritual phenomenon.

The crucifixion of our Lord, by those who rejected Him, was spiritually motivated and legally executed. Man is spiritually or personally constituted to be self-expressive, positively or negatively, good or evil. Faith and unbelief are spiritual in character. The chief priests and elders persuaded the multitudes against Jesus. The trial of Jesus before Caiaphas, the high priest, was nothing short of mockery. The spirit of unbelief pervaded their hearts. Jesus was charged with blasphemy and found guilty by His accusers. "Crucify Him" (Luke 23:21) was the cry of the Jews.

Israel was a subjugated nation under the jurisdiction of Rome, so they led Him to Pilate, who was governor of Judea, and made their accusations of Jesus before him. Pilate gave them a hearing and questioned Jesus. He could not prevail over their spirited aggression. Pilate, being politically astute, when he heard that Jesus was a Galilean, sent Him to Herod under whose jurisdiction He was subject. Herod heard Him gladly, but concurred with Pilate in his judgment of the case, and sent Him back to Pilate. The two, who before were enemies, were made friends. Pilate, bolstered by Herod's support, ordered the Roman soldiers to deliver Jesus to be crucified. With the allowance made by Pilate, Caiaphas immediately ordered the crucifixion of Jesus. Unbelief, literally, put Jesus to death. Simultaneously, in the same circumstance, the spirit of unbelief and the spirit of faith found expression in contrast:

the Jews in unbelief rejected Jesus, and Jesus in faith was spiritually laying down His life in His mission to redeem fallen man as He had throughout His whole humiliation. He was fulfilling His stewardship in keeping with the will of God.

Those who rejected Jesus didn't know the grave of His mortal body couldn't hold Him. God raised Him the third day. In His resurrection the mortal put on immortality—His glorified body. When nearing the cross, Jesus prayed, "And now, O Father, glorify thou me with thine own self with the glory which I had with thee before the world was" (John 17:5). If He hadn't had a glorious relationship with the Father in the spiritual manhood He assumed in eternity, before assuming His mortal manhood in time, this prayer would be without meaning.

The coming of our Lord into the world to redeem fallen man was a mission of faith motivated by love. His personal characteristics in His human nature are the same as in His Divine nature. In assuming His mortal body, His love is made manifest in human terms, with which man can relate. In reading the life of Jesus from the Gospels, one can readily discern the love Jesus has for those in all walks of life. Surely one would not want to be excluded.

When one learns of another's love, there is a magnetic drawing to that one. This is true in romance in anticipation of being complete in each other. The wonderful part of being complete in Jesus is that it is not just for time, but for eternity. Even Jesus anticipated a more glorious relationship with the Father in eternity that He couldn't have had in the confines of His mortal manhood. Think of how much more this is true of every one of us, shackled with the infirmities of one's mortal body and one's depraved nature.

In the circumstance of the crucifixion, the love of Jesus was made manifest to the uttermost in the fulfilling of His stewardship to redeem fallen man, a spiritual mission executed by faith and motivated by love. His whole humiliation was marked by the laying down of His life for the sheep continually, that He might share His life with all whose faith in Him is motivated by love for God. Furthermore, in His crucifixion, the legal and the spiritual are in contrast, but simultaneous by circumstance. The crucifixion of Jesus killed His mortal body, but not His spirit. While still body and spirit, hanging on the cross, He was in charge, and dismissed His spirit into the hands of the Father.

He is victor over the grave. This gives assurance to all believers that they too will have a glorified body in eternity. All will experience mortal death. It is the termination of the life cycle: the putting off of the mortal to assume the immortal, which will be experienced in eternity by all believers.

The contrasting potentials of faith and unbelief, resident in every heart, are made manifest in the circumstance of the crucifixion of Jesus: the potential of faith to believe God under the most trying circumstance, and the potential of unbelief in God to murder the Son of God as demonstrated by Israel (Acts 7:52).

God is reconciled to man. "All sin shall be forgiven the sons of men" (Mark 3:28). The Gospel or the good news bids man to be reconciled to God by faith in Jesus, faith motivated by love for God. The reconciliation of God to man and of man to God creates a living bond wherein one is married to the Son of God, adopted by the Father, and made a joint heir with Jesus to all the glories the kingdom of God holds. All believers collectively are the bride of Jesus. My reader, be responsive to God's love, to the bid of the good news, and live to God's glory!

THE WILL OF GOD

The Will of God
Part I

God's will is spiritual in character. It addresses one's person and one's office: one's character and one's stewardship. One is to be personally upright in keeping with the character of God, and officially faithful in the stewardship of God's appointment. God's Standard of Righteousness, God's Righteous Order, and God's Recompensing Judgments are all-inclusive of the will of God, and will be addressed in that order.

Man is a created personality, social, and family-oriented. God's objective in having created man was to share His life with man, the infinite with the finite. The will of God is God's means in preparing man in time to fit into the family of God in eternity. Family life, subject to the will of God in time, is a prototype of the family of God in eternity.

The man and the woman are constituted to be complementary to each other in the execution of their respective offices. Instinctively, both have a consciousness of being, in gender, complete in a family bond with the other. When first complete in a personal bond to Jesus, they will be kindred in spirit with each other. Home can be so great!

The subject of the home will be addressed in chapter three, under God's Righteous Order.

One can be knowledgeable of the will of God, committed to doing what is required of one, and yet be objectively impersonal, self-serving. Doing the will of God is character building and commendable, but it will not effect a living bond to God. When one's response to the will of God is motivated by love for God, one's way of life will exemplify a living bond to God. One's caring spirit for God and for others will be objectively personal, not self-serving.

The will of God is directional to man wherein he can enjoy his greatest freedom. Sin, excluding God and exalting self, enslaves man to sin. I want my reader to be as God created man to be, with a purpose in life to be to God's praise and to enjoy the fullness of a life motivated by love for God.

All need to solicit guidance from God, like a child who needs parental help in making personal choices. "If any of you lack wisdom, let him ask of God, that giveth to all men liberally, and upbraideth not; and it shall be given him" (James 1:5). One who asks of God will be given enablement to discern the wisdom given by God. Prayer fellowship with God is living in the spirit of worship, like the communion shared by a faithful husband and wife living in the spirit of devotion. The loss of communication distances one from the other, also one from God. "Pray without ceasing" (1 Thess. 5:17); live in the spirit of worship. As one lives in the consciousness of the Father's love, one is constrained to walk uprightly.

God's will is a moral issue. The dictionary defines morals as relating principles of right and wrong behavior. This definition licenses one to make the determination. However, all of manhood is subject to the standard of righteousness authored by God. No code of morals can excel that which reveals the moral glory of God for which man was created. God says, "I have created him for my glory" (Isa. 43:7). Situation morals are without spiritual value; are an accommodation to circumstances that licenses sin. Don't let yielding to temptation derail you from God's Standard of Righteousness!

The will and the objective of God go together like the rules and the objective of a game. The one does not make sense apart from the other. The ultimate objective of God is the establishment of a spiritual kingdom. Included are all the redeemed in functional harmony with the glory of God. The will of God is the basis of spiritually preparing or maturing man unto this end. In principle, it is like the training of children in the home to be responsible stewards in a home of their own. As children in the home are being prepared for a higher calling, so the sons of God in time are being prepared for a higher calling in eternity.

"'For this is the covenant that I will make with the house of Israel after those days,' saith the Lord; 'I will put my laws into their mind, and write them in their hearts: and I will be to them a God, and they shall be to me a people: and they shall not teach every man his neighbour, and every man his brother, saying, "Know the Lord:" for all shall know me, from the least to the greatest'" (Heb. 8:10-11). The kingdom of God, the kingdom of heaven, the family of God, the household of faith, the body of Christ, are all the same spiritual entity. The kingdom of His dear Son is in contrast to the kingdom of this world wherein the spirit of antichrist reigns.

The kingdom of God is a spiritual or living entity that endures forever. Every member is a functional part. "For as the body is one, and hath many members, and all the members of that body, being many, are one body, so also is Christ" (1 Cor. 12:12). A spiritual kingdom is not divisible by time or locale. "Thy will be done in earth as it is in heaven" (Matt. 6:10).

For one who is responsive to God's love, one's priority in life is to be found pleasing to God. One will lay down his life for Jesus. "For whosoever will save his life shall lose it; and whosoever will lose his life for my sake shall find it" (Matt. 16:25). Cross-bearing is not executed by a determination of the will alone, but in the spontaneity of faith motivated by love for God—a response of the whole man. The principle of cross-bearing is like a godly mother who literally gives of herself continually for the sake of her family. The personal cost isn't counted because it is motivated by love. The sharing of her life is not reckoned in terms of sacrifice. "If any man will come after me, let him deny himself, and take up his cross daily, and follow me" (Luke 9:23).

The will of God regarding righteousness is the same for everyone. God has but one standard of righteousness. One's stewardship, which is a part of the will of God, is by God's appointment. What is stewardship? In context, stewardship is the assuming of official responsibility in the appointments of God: for example, the man to his manhood and the woman to her womanhood. Innate aptitudes, gifts, and talents instinctively make one's stewardship come natural.

One has latitude in the will of God to make personal choices within ordained bounds. One can buy the car of one's choice as long as one can afford it, and be within family accord.

The will of God is not to be equated with circumstances. It is spiritual, or personal, in character; circumstances are impersonal. Sometimes it is hard to think of the personal, the spiritual, apart from the impersonal, from circumstances. They are so directly associated in one's mind. There are those who think that in some way all circumstances are within the will of God.

One who has sinned against God and repents with contrite heart, and comes to know the Lord, will reason that what was allowed to happen was by God's permissive will. This kind of reasoning is inadvertently self-serving and is without spiritual value. God does not have two wills, a direct and a permissive will. The latter would make God a party to one's sin, allowing evil that good might come. God has but one will and objective for man. There will be personal and official distinctions, but all are subject to the one will of God.

Circumstances, even those that are providential, are not to be equated with the will of God. It is not the circumstances themselves, but the spirit in which one faces them that reveals how much one is kindred in spirit to the will of God. One cannot always differentiate between an ordinary circumstance and a providential circumstance. The will of God, on the other hand, is not that mysterious, but revelation to man of being as God created man to be. Was it the will of God when circumstances led Joseph to be jailed by Pharaoh, or was the will of God to be honored in those circumstances? Circumstances do not alter the personal and official responsibilities one has in honoring the will of God. Being given to the will of God is an exercise of faith. Faith is spiritual in character, and when motivated by love, lifts one above the press of circumstances. Hunger does not license one to steal. When the truth will convict, one does not have license to lie. No circumstance licenses one to profane the will of God.

All circumstances are a consequence of something that happened. The first question asked when appraising a circumstance is, "How did it happen?" The cause is not always readily known, and perhaps may never be known. It can be of one's own making. Providential circumstances are of God's making, and always carry a message from Him. The message can be the assurance of God's hand on one's life, of His caring love, the revealing to one of his personal relationship to God, and possibly a directive from God regarding one's stewardship. The circumstance will obviously be of God's making and the message it bears will trigger a spontaneous response from whoever is attuned to God: it even carries a spiritual quickening of one's consciousness of God as the circumstance is related; it doesn't lessen with time. Others may witness the circumstance and not get the message, as it was with those who journeyed with the Apostle Paul on the Damascus road. Suddenly there shone about him a light from heaven. The circumstance carried a message from God that he alone received. Those who traveled with him were witnesses and stood speechless, hearing a voice, but seeing no man. We do not know the spiritual impact the circumstance had on their lives, but the testimony of Paul couldn't have been without spiritual significance to them.

There are many circumstances of providence recorded in the Scriptures: the plagues on Egypt; the burning bush that got the attention of Moses; Shadrach, Meshach, and Abednego in the fiery furnace and the form of a fourth like unto the Son of God, carrying a message to Nebuchadnezzar, king of Babylon. The circumstance dreamed by Belshazzar, son of Nebuchadnezzar, carried a message from God: the handwriting on the wall deeply troubled him, but, even worse, neither he nor his masterminds had the spiritual discernment to interpret the writing. Daniel, known to be a man of God, a Jew exiled from Judah, was brought before the king to interpret the writing, which he did. Not any of the above who were personally involved would try to explain away providential circumstances by phenomena of nature. Providential circumstances are not spiritual in character, but are directly associated with the message they bear, which is spiritual in character.

Providential circumstances are not to be equated with the will of God. The will of God is spiritual or personal in character, circumstances are impersonal in character: circumstances of providence always carry a message from God. They have the distinction of being associated with the message they bear, which doesn't fade with time, but leaves a lasting impression on one's memory. The many I have experienced always effected a spiritual quickening in my heart and gave present evidence to me of God's hand on my life. I will relate one circumstance that is self-evidently providential.

It was near the close of a week of meetings I was having at the First Baptist Church of Gladstone, Oregon. The attendance had been good. My ministry was warmly received. The pastor of the church was a godly man and dedicated to his calling. He was giving thought to his ministry in the days to follow. He wanted to carry on the work of God that had been so obviously enkindled in the hearts of his people. He asked me if I had any suggestions. I told him that when hearts are tender toward God, they are open to learn of God's Standard of Righteousness. Surprisingly few have knowledge of the Ten Commandments other than from a legal premise. They hold so much more when taught from a spiritual premise.

To my knowledge, the best work on the "Ten Commandments" was authored by Ezekiel Hopkins, born 1633. However, there are no doubt later authors who have written on the subject whose works are worthy of review. I asked the pastor, "Is there a book store that carries used religious books in Portland, probably windfalls from old estates?" He said that there were, but that they were not shelved by any classified order; we would probably find what they had piled on the floor at the rear of the store. I told him that was usually the case, but also an indication of the market for old religious books. We drove to the store and found the pile of religious books in the rear of the store as he had predicted. I started searching through the books. I found a rather old book, the color of its cover faded with age. It was titled, *The Ten Commandments* by Ezekiel Hopkins. I didn't even know that it had ever been published in one volume. My copy was about three hundred pages of Volume I of a set of three volumes on the works of Ezekiel Hopkins.

We looked at each other in amazement, realizing at that very minute we had witnessed a circumstance of providence, and the message it carried was directed to us. It was an assurance of God's benediction on the plans of ministry we were making and a token of the enablement He would be giving in the days ahead. This was an extraordinary visitation of God that neither of us will ever forget.

The treatment of the subject by Ezekiel Hopkins was enlightening to the pastor and an adjunct to his ministry in the weeks that followed. He has since loaned the book to several pastors, who in turn have shared the spiritual value it holds with their respective congregations.

Providential circumstances, when related, hold one's interest, make evident the reality of the spiritual world of which we clearly are all a part. There is a quickening of one's personal thoughts of God, which sobers one to give more thought to the place God is given in one's own heart.

The will of God will be entertained under three subheads; namely, God's Standard of Righteousness, God's Righteous Order, and God's Recompensing Judgments.

God's Standard of Righteousness
Part II

God's Standard of Righteousness is the ethic for man, epitomized in the Ten Commandments and further addressed in the Sermon on the Mount. They are like positive precepts, and are directional to man's greatest freedom; they are instructional to man in coming to know the tenets of righteousness. They are first like a schoolmaster to one in coming to know Christ. When the spirit of love for God pervades one's heart, there is no longer a need of a schoolmaster. The Commandments become life principles in the hearts of those who are responsive to God.

The Commandments are essentially spiritual in character, not legal. They enlist a personal response, and have an objective beyond what the law can effect. God did not create man to enslave him to a legal system, but that he might be free in a living bond to Himself and to all believers.

The fall did not change the way man was constituted. All of man's faculties were impaired, but still functioned. By the interaction of the intellect, the emotions, the conscience, and the will, the disposition of the heart finds expression, the response of the integrated personality, the whole man. When God said, "My son, give me thine heart" (Prov. 23:26), He was addressing the whole man.

The Ten Commandments, written on tablets of stone by the finger of God for Israel to observe, were in essence written in the hearts of the Gentiles, inclusive of all peoples. Man has never lost a natural proclivity Godward.

Man has an innate consciousness of spiritual kinship to God, of the image of God he was created to bear. It surfaces as one learns of God. When the revelation God is giving of

Himself comes into the focal range of faith, it enlists a personal response.

It comes natural for parents to share their concepts of God with their children. It does not require doctrinal knowledge of the Scriptures to teach a child of God's love and of God's Standard of Righteousness. It will bear witness to what is already in one's heart. It is by precept and example that what is taught becomes revelation. The spirit that pervades the home, and the shared thoughts of God, become the strongest influence in one's life. One is indoctrinated in the religion espoused by one's parents.

God's Standard of Righteousness is woven into the fabric of all religions. This ethical kinship to Israel gives reason for one to pattern his relationship to God in terms of the Old Covenant: of being blessed for obedience and cursed for disobedience. The threat of the consequences of one's disobedience prods one to walk uprightly, and in context effects a self-righteousness. Even one's self-image may be an appraisal of one's own spiritual status, but from a legal premise, not spiritual (or personal) in character. Being given to the law may or may not effect a spiritual or personal relationship to God.

I must remind my reader that the Old Covenant was made with the nation, Israel, with all Israelites collectively. When the spirit of disobedience prevailed in Israel, the judgment fell upon all collectively, the disobedient and the obedient alike. All Israelites, individually, are spiritually or personally related to God, as is all of manhood, and will suffer a personal loss as a consequence of one's own sin, not punishment.

Keeping the laws of God is commendable; effects a good relationship with others; dignifies one's person; and gains respect and trust from family and friends. However, keeping God's laws is self-serving unless motivated by a love for God and man. Inadvertently, one can be in bondage to a legal system, and not be personally responsive to God as man was created to be.

One's thoughts of God, by the way his mind has been programmed, may or may not be the whole truth. It is well to remember this as it keeps one's mind open to having one's thoughts of God challenged. One's knowledge of God comes from a progressive unveiling of the revelation that God is giving of Himself.

One who is interested enough to ask questions on the Word of God is spiritually motivated to know the truth. In the Gospel of Mark, it is recorded how Jesus silenced the Sadducees on the subject of the resurrection. A Pharisee, one of the scribes, having heard our Lord's reasoning, perceived that He answered them well. This man was a lawyer whose service within the scribes was the interpretation of the Law. He asked Jesus a question, "Which is the first commandment of all?" (Mark 12:28). In the context there is no suggestion of any subtle intent. He was seeking the truth in a right spirit. "And Jesus answered him, 'the first of all the commandments is, Hear, O Israel; the Lord our God is one Lord: And thou shalt love the Lord thy God with all thy heart and with all thy soul, and with all thy mind, and with all thy strength: this is the first commandment. And the second is like, namely this, Thou shalt love thy neighbor as thyself. There is none other commandment greater than these.' And the scribe said unto him, 'Well, Master, thou hast said the truth: for there is one God; and there is none other but he: And to love him with all the heart, and with all the understanding, and with all the soul, and with all the strength, and to love his neighbor as himself, is more than all whole burnt offerings and sacrifices.' And when Jesus saw that he answered discreetly, he said unto him, 'Thou are not far from the kingdom of God.' And no man after that durst ask him any question" (Mark 12:29-34).

There must have been a spiritual quickening in the lawyer's heart, for one whose thoughts had trafficked in the legal to have readily entertained the words of our Lord. The letter of the law is a driving force to comply, and gives the obeyer of the law wherein to boast, but does not enrich him spiritually. The spirit of the law invites a personal response motivated by love for God and man. All parties involved are spiritually enriched by the laying down of their lives for one another, that is essential to a living bond. For example: when the caresses of a mother's touch are felt by a child, it quickens a responsive love in the heart of the child for the mother. The same is true as one learns of the love of God for him. It enkindles an endearment in his heart for God. The love of God constrains one to walk uprightly.

Man's conscience makes him sensitive to moral values in keeping with what he has been taught. Its function is spiritual in character, not legal. It warns, like a sensor, when wrongdoing is being entertained, but does not threaten. Although fallen man is dead to a living bond to God, his conscience is attuned to God. God is sending a message of life to man. Don't miss it!

Conscience must be enlightened to be trustworthy. Man is to heed conscience, but also must keep what he holds to be the truth open to challenge. God has not left man without the guidelines of righteousness. The Decalogue was given to Israel at Mt. Sinai as a part of their covenant with God. The basic tenets were not new nor exclusive to Israel. They were in keeping with the character of God and befitted man created in the image of God. As far back as history is recorded, the moral content of the Decalogue has been the ethical standard of man. The records of Hammurabi, which preceded the records of Moses, bear testimony to this antiquity. The moral code of the three great monotheistic religions, Islam, Judaism, and Christianity, has the ethic mark of agreement. All three stem from Abraham. The God of Abraham is the same yesterday, today, and forever.

Much has been written on the Decalogue with wise instruction that is available for study. It will be found that the Ten Commandments are a concentrate of moral precepts that are inexhaustible in their coverage of human behavior. They are worthy of careful scrutiny and diligent study. Much moral direction is included that may be missed without competent tutelage.

Man must be enlightened to the revelation of God's caring love for him, to see the excellencies of the glory of God. "No man can come to me, except the Father . . . draw him" (John 6:44). This is by the magnetic power of God's love, effecting a personal response in the heart of man for God. It is the writer's opinion that when one is desirous of knowing God, God will bring circumstances to pass wherein He is made known. The circumstance of Philip and the Ethiopian eunuch (Acts 8:26-40) is more than coincidental. It took a Damascus Road experience for the Apostle Paul to see the Lord. Righteousness becomes revelation to the seeker after God; it is the goal as one pursues knowledge of God.

When one is taught the ethic of righteousness, conscience is conditioned to reject substandards. The reader will recall the look from our Lord that caught the eye of Peter at the time of his denial (Luke 22:61-62). The message was a communiqué of righteousness. Peter was melted into repentance and embraced the Lord with renewed faith. How could a look from the Lord have had meaning apart from knowledge of what was expected?

The Decalogue is the basis of all moral instruction. Knowledge of it is as important to building character as mathematics is to engineering a bridge. It is God's standard for human behavior. One must be taught the commandments to have a knowledge of righteousness. What is academic by precept and example becomes revelation when exemplified in a life: by precept and example. Qualities of character such as integrity, dependability, punctuality, honoring propriety, orderliness, neatness, cleanliness, and respect for authority are all patent to righteousness.

The Sermon on the Mount transposes the letter of the law to the spirit of the law. The letter of the law says, "Thou shalt not commit adultery" (Matt. 5:27). The spirit of the law transposes this to say, "Whosoever looketh upon a woman to lust after her hath committed adultery with her already in his heart" (Matt. 5:28). One who is of a kindred spirit with Christ will not entertain evil. "Walk in the Spirit, and ye shall not fulfill the lust of the flesh" (Gal. 5:16). Depravity in the heart may assert itself by exciting lust. This in itself is not sin, but a surfacing of the depraved man. It is when lust is entertained that it becomes sinful (James 1:13-15).

The spirit of the law is declared by our Lord in the Beatitudes. It finds expression in those who are the poor in spirit, the meek, the merciful, the pure in heart, the peacemakers, and those who are persecuted for righteousness sake. There is no greater excellency known to man than in being Godlike in spirit. ". . . Now if any man have not the Spirit of Christ, he is none of his" (Rom. 8:9).

In the Sermon on the Mount our Lord said, "Think not that I am come to destroy the law, or the prophets: I am not come to destroy but to fulfill" (Matt. 5:17). The spirit of the law is attuned to life-giving principles. The letter of the law is academic before it becomes revelation, before there can be a personal response that stems from the heart. "For the law was given by Moses, but grace and truth came by Jesus Christ" (John 1:17).

The Law given by Moses was all-inclusive of the Old Covenant. It was like a contract between God and Israel, submitted by God through Moses and ratified in unison by Israel. The Ten Commandments were the ethic of the Old Covenant. They were essentially spiritual in a legal context, just as the taking of an oath is in a court of law. The spirit in which the covenant was executed revealed their hearts: God's heart for Israel and Israel's heart for God. God's objective in the Covenant was not only the revelation of Himself to Israel, but to all peoples.

The Old Covenant was made with Israel collectively, en masse, as also were God's promises of blessings for keeping covenant and curses for breaking covenant. Both took effect according to current circumstances and were temporal in duration. God's election of Israel to be His people was administrative in character. It was an expansion of the priesthood ordained by God to national status, the Levites officiating. It gave theocratic distinction to Israel. The relationship between God and His people afforded a revelation of God's heart to the children of Israel and to all peoples. It bore testimony to the whole world of the only true and living God. The message has never been lost, not even to this day, to those who will carefully read Israel's place in sacred history. The principles of righteousness have never changed; nor has God's love for man.

Israel's covenant identity with God was pivotal in their worship of Him, as marital bonds are pivotal on the devotion between husband and wife. Faithfulness in worship motivated by a love for God would be giving an Israelite a higher calling, that of being brought into a personal living bond with God. Breaking covenant gave cause for deep consternation and moved the guilty to repent and bring a sin offering to the priest for forgiveness and restoration to covenant identity. No greater fear gripped an Israelite's heart than the fear of being cut off from covenant identity. To him it would have meant being cut off from God.

The Law and the Covenant are of the same legal content and are used interchangeably. The Law addressed the terms of the Covenant and covered every phase of one's life: worship, domestic, and civic. Sin had dulled man's consciousness of righteousness and of God's objective in having created man.

The Law was academic not only to Israel in learning what is entailed in God's Standard of Righteousness, but in principle to all of manhood. The Old Covenant was single to Israel, excluding all Gentile nations. The terms of the Covenant were legal in character, administered by ordained authority vested by God. The Law commanded compliance and decreed judgments but could not dictate the motivation of one's responses. The Law had no jurisdiction over the spiritual man, the responses that stem from one's heart. The law addressed the terms of the covenant, what an Israelite was to do and not to do, innate instincts concurring. All of manhood is subject to the principles of righteousness from infancy. Man is taught moral values, right from wrong, ordinate and inordinate behavior, but motivation determines the spiritual or personal value in their execution.

When the rich young ruler asked our Lord what good thing could he do to inherit eternal life, Jesus quoted the last six commandments that are directional to man as he relates to man. The young man's reply was that he had kept all of these from his youth. Our Lord said to him, "One thing thou lackest" (Mark 10:21). The only logical deduction one can make is that his observance of the commandments had not been motivated by love, and was not in the spirit of laying down his life for God or for man. The first commandment of them all, given by Jesus in answer to the lawyer's question (quoted earlier), would apply in the execution of all the commandments. Love is essential in a living or personal bond to God and to each other.

By hearing over and over again the Biblical account of Israel in covenant identity with God, of God's faithfulness in fulfilling His promises, and of the prophets voicing the word of God with strong pleas to Israel to keep covenant, one's mind is being programmed to think in the same terms that God had with Israel: favorable circumstances for obedience to God's Standard of Righteousness and curses for disobedience. While it makes for a better life to live within the bounds of righteousness, it does not necessarily imply a personal relationship with God.

Israel was collectively related to God by covenant on legal terms that were conditional in character. God's relationship to an individual, Jew and Gentile alike, is spiritual or personal in character. In adversity, one will often ponder where he got off track or missed the turn: his current problem in his mind is conditional upon what he had or hadn't done: this would be a legal appraisal of his circumstance. One's personal relationship to God is spiritual in character and will be in keeping with the endearment for God one has in one's heart: circumstances are not relevant.

The difference between the personal and the legal as one relates to God is easily garbled in one's logic. One's logic may be reasonable and yet not the truth, but the truth will always be logical and reasonable. One will reason that what God did for Israel, He will do for him, knowing that God is not a respecter of persons. He is thinking in the realm of the tangible, of the benefits, and is unmindful that the benefits are conditional upon the terms of a covenant with God in which he has no part. Furthermore, he reasons that God's forgiveness of Israel's sin on the day of Atonement also applies to God's forgiveness of his own sins. He associates his personal relationship to God with Israel's legal identity to God. Again, he mistakes the personal for the legal. The consequences of sin, the personal losses suffered, are not in the context of the legal mind, therefore the subject is not addressed. It is true that forgiven sin will be remembered against no one forever, but forgiveness does not negate the personal losses one suffers as a consequence of sin. One will live with the consequences of his sin.

In orthodox Christianity, one is taught from childhood that he is born under a penal judgment of death on sin, that Jesus paid the penalty of his sin by dying on the cross in his stead, vicariously. His mind is inadvertently being programmed to think from a legal premise as he relates to God. He grows into adulthood comforted by what God has done for him, and what He will do for him, completely oblivious to the fact that it is self-serving, possibly void of a responsive love to God's love for him. In a subtle way, he is a victim of circumstances; his thoughts of God are correlated with Israel's covenant identity with God. This is understandable, as so much of sacred history is in the context of the Old Covenant. I will give the following as an example: The prophet Micah, who was contemporary with Isaiah, prophesied under Jotham, Asa, and Hezekiah, kings of Judah. In the book of Micah, Micah quoted words of Balaam, spoken several hundred years earlier. Balaam's poetic gift found expression in prophetic words. He prophesied in the days of Moses when Israel was possessing the promised land, and in the context of Israel having routed the Amorites and caused fear to grip the hearts of the Moabites, Ammonites, and the Midianites. "He hath shewed thee, O man, what is good; and what doth the Lord require of thee, but to do justly, and to love mercy, and to walk humbly with thy God?" (Mic. 6:8). This quote and others of Balaam are frequently quoted today, some twenty-seven hundred years later. They were spoken under the terms of the Old Covenant. As they are heard over and over again, one's mind is being programmed to think from the same premise. One might ask in exclamation, "What more could be asked of man than to do what is required of him!" The answer is "Nothing." The Law does not address one's spiritual relationship to God. The Law was weak in that it could not exact a responsive love to God's love for one. Motivation determines the spiritual value of everything one does; even faith in God that is not motivated by love for God is not saving faith, cannot create a living bond to God. The Apostle Paul asked the Galatians, "Is the law then against the promises of God? God forbid: for if there had been a law given which could have given life, verily righteousness should have been by the law" (Gal. 3:21).

God's objective in having created man was to share His life with man. It is a spiritual objective and cannot be fulfilled by legal means. However, the Law was not against the promises of God. It is to man's advantage in every way to stay within the bounds of God's Standard of Righteousness, but he will never have God's fulfillment of purpose for him apart from a living bond to God.

One's life is revealing of the kind of person he or she is as they relate to God and to each other.

God's Administrative Order of Righteousness Part III

God's Righteous Order will be addressed briefly in each of the three institutions ordained by God: the Home, the Church, and the State. "The powers that be are ordained by God" (Rom. 13:1) for man's good and to God's glory. Man is the beneficiary. The same was true of the Sabbath Day. "Man was not created for the Sabbath, but the Sabbath for man" (Mark 2:27).

All objectives of God end in Himself. "All things were created by Him, and for Him" (Col. 1:16). How wonderful it is for man to have the potential of being spiritually bonded to and energized by the infinite One, a potential that gives man a status above all personalities God has created.

God is the ultimate of all spiritual values. Man has the unique distinction in creation of being created in the image of God and able to share in His life. "I have created him for my glory, I have formed him, yea, I have made him" (Isa. 43:7).

God's Righteous Order is administrative in character, subjecting man to official stewardship under ordained authority. The Home and the Church are spiritual entities. One's identity with them is a personal involvement. The place in one's heart for God and for family will determine the spiritual climate in the Home and in the Church. The State is a legal entity, vested with power and authority to maintain righteousness in society. One is subject to civil government whether his heart is in it or not.

Inasmuch as all three institutions are of God, the righteous principles that apply to one will also apply to the others. They will be in keeping with the character of God. Each one is a separate entity, but all three are interrelated and interdependent. Each one has delegated head-ship with vested authority. All are subject to the one God. This allows no room for impropriety. The Church is not to have the preeminence over the other two, but God is to have the preeminence in all three. All three are subject to God's Standard of Righteousness, which is epitomized in the Ten Commandments.

The Home will be the first of the three institutions addressed. It is the basic unit of society and can be a foretaste of heaven, a prelude of the family of God in eternity. God in His sovereignty elected the man and the woman to their respective offices, the man to his manhood and the woman to her womanhood. They were genetically constituted and endowed with gifts and graces to make them complementary to each other. In marital bonds, the twain become one flesh, one entity, the Home. In the Home, the husband and wife can experience full expression of their respective offices to the endearment of each other and to the respect of their children.

The man has weighty responsibilities in the execution of his priestly office. He is to be knowledgeable of the revelation God is giving of Himself. The priesthood of the Home has never been abrogated. It isn't an optional matter with him, but a part of his stewardship by the election of God. He is to officiate family worship. In my thinking, this entails a time together in the spirit of worship and in formally focusing all thoughts objectively on God. When family worship has not been in one's life, the man, in the office of priest, may feel intimidated, unworthy, and out of place, but God will give the enablement. He will feel God's support in the first steps of faith he takes in executing his office. It is amazing the spiritual impact one has when the convictions of his heart to please God find expression. The response he gets from his family is so rewarding. It stimulates him to be more knowledgeable of the Bible, to know the continuity of its message: God's love made manifest in the revelation He gives of Himself, culminating in Jesus Christ. The message becomes rooted in his own heart as he shares it with his family. When God's love for one becomes revelation, it excites a responsive love for God. Love engenders a spiritual bond. It opens one's heart to commune with God. It is as natural for man to commune with God as it is for members of a family to commune with each other. Loss of communication distances them from each other. Keeping in touch is vital to living bonds. Those who lose communication are soon alienated. Reading the Word of God and praying together binds a family to God and to each other. It is a great way to start the day.

Family worship under the priesthood of the Home prepares hearts to be subject to collective worship under the priesthood of the Church. The sanctuary of worship will be hallowed with reverential respect for God. The pastor's message of the gospel will be one with which one can relate, because of what one has been taught at home.

The institution of the Home is greater than any one member. The Home not only perpetuates the race, but also fosters the culture. Children, for the most part, follow the example of their parents. The Home that does not teach children obedience and respect for righteousness is an incubator of crime. In the Home, the children are to be taught stewardship pertinent to their respective offices.

Ordained headship in the Home is delegated to the man. He is accountable to God to maintain family harmony in keeping with the spirit of righteousness, and to officiate family worship. All members of the family are subject to him within bounds of propriety. The woman is not demeaned by being subject to her own husband. Her respect for his office enkindles a like spirit in the hearts of the children and endears them all to each other: it no less puts the burden of responsible stewardship on the man. The husband

and the wife are endowed with all that is pertinent in the execution of their respective offices. When the honoring of them is motivated by a love for God and for each other, it will be a foretaste of celestial glory for which man is being prepared.

The writer desires to keep before the reader continually that the ultimate objective of the Will of God is to establish a spiritual kingdom of celestial glory in which all the redeemed are functionally integrated. Every believer is a part of this kingdom now, and is being prepared to take his place of service in eternity.

The election of the man and the woman to their respective offices is strictly administrative. The man who doesn't assume the responsibilities of his office is derelict in his stewardship. "But if any man provide not for his own, and especially for those of his own house, he hath denied the faith, and is worse than an infidel" (1 Tim. 5:8).

The husband and wife are equally responsible for creating a quality of life in the home that can be cherished. When one is taught from his youth to share in the workload of the home, it will become a way of life and strengthen his character. When the spirit of love for God and for each other pervades the home, it will be Home Sweet Home. Within these bonds, parents can share spiritual values with their children effectively. It is by precept and example that what is taught makes sense and invites a personal involvement in like manner. It is frustrating for children to be taught principles of righteousness that are not exemplified in the lives of their parents. The direction and training a child receives at home will influence the kind of person he will be in the Church and in the civil world.

When the man and the woman are committed to their respective offices, they will have dignity, self respect, and respect for each other to the glory of God. This is right preparation for being good husbands and wives, and for being good fathers and mothers. When the office is honored, God is being honored. The Apostle Paul said, "I magnify my office" (Rom. 11:13).

The stewardship of the man and the woman is for time only. There will be no marrying or giving in marriage in glory, but all will be as the angels (Matt. 22:30). Faithful stewardship in time is preparation for one's place in the kingdom of God in eternity. There is nothing more revealing of character and faithful stewardship than one's track record. It is never lost. Only God can evaluate it righteously, for He alone knows all that is involved in one's life: what has been transmitted through the genes, the effects of circumstances, and the spiritual status of one's heart. Motivation determines the spiritual value of all actions; whatever is not motivated by love for God or man is self-serving.

Godly parents will want to share their knowledge of God with their children, not only by telling them of God's love for them, but by citing evidence with which they can relate. This will excite a responsive love for God that is almost spontaneous. The more the love of God for one becomes revelation, the more God is endeared to one's heart. There will be an ever present consciousness of His love that will constrain one to walk uprightly. This doesn't just happen. God fearing parents, by precept and example, and disciplinary measures when needed, are effectual in a child coming to know God and His righteousness. "This is the work of God, that ye believe on Him whom He hath sent" (John 6:29).

A father and mother who are kindred in spirit with Jesus will be kindred in spirit with each other and will engender a kindred spirit in the hearts of their children. As a child grows older, his consciousness of God's love and parental trust strengthens his moral fabric and his sense of responsibility and accountability.

In the environment of the Home, wherein God is given the preeminence, the work of the Holy Spirit in a child's heart is readily effectual. One's innate proclivity for God surfaces early. He is responsive to the message of God's love for him mediated through caring parents. When one's gifts, talents, and instinctive aptitudes begin to find expression, discerning parents will give words of encouragement in exercising and developing them unto worthy stewardship.

This means that a child's time will be occupied constructively: it is for one's good, as was exemplified when "God took Adam and put him into the garden of Eden to dress it and to keep it" (Gen. 2:15). A child must be given responsibility in the workload of the home befitting one's age and gender. The giving of oneself with eagerness to help is given encouragement by the kind of spirit issuing from one's parents. Love begets love and invites a helping hand. A pushy and censoring manner in getting a child to work is more apt to create rebellion in the child's heart and discord in the family. On the other hand, being overprotective of the child inadvertently weakens him in character, makes him more dependent, and possibly licenses the child to use one parent over the other. A father and mother must assume the responsibility of their respective offices in keeping family harmony. When they are respectful of each other, they will have the respect of their children. The Home can be in complete disarray when a child is allowed to take over.

The responsibility parents have in holding the reins that lead a child's life is awesome. It takes the wisdom that is from above to balance the exercising of restraint and the giving of freedom in what will best serve the child in the kind of person and steward he is becoming.

One is affected by one's depraved nature and is prone to think of self first; being socially constituted, one craves the company and attention of others. Only love, and the caring attention of another for one, can temper a selfish disposition. The care of the baby by someone who is just doing her job is not enough to satisfy that innate craving in one's heart for love. He soon learns to cry for the attention he wants at the time. As this is repeated over and over again, that which serves selfish ends becomes one's way of life. It is the phenomenon of making a spoiled child. He can possibly become calloused to love and care that doesn't serve his ends. The responses to another's love that are self-serving have no spiritual values to enrich one's life.

It can be so different when a child has the loving attention of both parents who are respectful of each other. The love parents have for each other engenders a kindred spirit in the child for its parents. The child will want to be a part of the action, and with encouragement and direction will respond with a helping hand, not for pay, but in the spirit of giving of oneself in response to parental love. Words of praise and appreciation from the parents are positive incentives for the child to do his work well and with pride. An allowance adequate for meeting the child's personal needs is the responsibility of the parents. It keeps their relationship in the home spiritual in character, out of the market place and the temptation to be self-serving: it makes children responsible in sharing the workload of the home.

Parental guidance is crucial to a child in his/her adolescent years. Positive precepts also carry the weight of the negative. Parents are responsible to warn and caution their children of the personal loss one suffers as a consequence of sin: to keep a child from being spiritually maimed for the rest of his life. Sin dwarfs one's heart for God; blights one's spiritual stature; and affects the kind of person one is becoming. Most damaging is that sin alienates one from God.

When the spirit of love for God and for one another pervades the home, a spiritual bond is being forged that makes for congenial interaction between parents and their children. Wise counsel is most apt to be received. A child who has been taught abstinence and brought up to be respectful of oneself and of others, and to honor God's Standard of Righteousness in faithful stewardship, is prepared for what has been latent in one's life prior to reaching the age of puberty. If one's body chemistry and biological urges have not been balanced by spiritual values, one could be on the brink of being a casualty in one's own life.

The boy and the girl in their respective homes are apprentices in the election of God to official stewardship. Both are endowed with the essentials pertinent to making them complementary to each other in a home of their own. Not until they near the age of puberty does an innate affinity for each other surface. It excites a natural romance between them that will test the spiritual values they have been taught. When kept within ordinate bounds, it will hold memories that will be cherished throughout their lives. Being kindred in spirit with God while they are single is a prerequisite for being of a kindred spirit with each other in their marriage. When God is given the preeminence in their home, it can be a foretaste of heaven.

Great responsibility falls on parental stewardship. Reverence for God and respect for each other becomes a way of life to those who love God. The spirit that pervades the home will find expression in the lives of the children. In years to come, the culture of their childhood home will be a prototype of the kind of home they establish as an adult. When God is revered and all members of the family are endeared to each other, home will hold cherished memories.

The second institution to be addressed under God's Righteous Order is The Institution of Worship, better known as the Church. While the family finds embodiment in the Home, collective families find embodiment in the Church.

It was in the heart of God in creating man to be in communion with man in a family bond like unto the Divine family. On the seventh day, having ended His work of creation, He entered into His rest as an example for man to follow. He also exemplified the spirit in which it was to be observed. He blessed and sanctified the day. We learn from the Old Covenant the awesome holiness in which the day was hallowed.

After the fall of Adam and Eve, God ordained rituals of worship that prefigured in type the message of redemption, and were to be observed by them and their posterity until fulfilled in Jesus Christ.

Our Lord entered His rest on the first day of the week, the Lord's Day, after having fulfilled His mission of redemption, a finished work. All believers worship the risen Christ, their file leader. When Jesus was raised from the dead, the mortal body He assumed put on immortality, His glorified body. This is assurance to all believers that their mortal bodies shall also put on immortality, the redemption of the whole man, body and spirit. How wonderful to anticipate deliverance from one's depraved nature and one's mortal body: free to be functional in one's glorified body in the family of God for all eternity. Praise God! To have such a glorious life in the family of God in eternity is the fulfillment of God's objective in having created man: that He might share His life with man, the life of God mediated through the man, Christ Jesus.

The local church is the embodiment of a group of believers, as the home is the embodiment of all members of the family. Any reference to the church includes all in the body of believers, as references to the home include all members in the family. However, the anointing of God is not on all local churches any more than God is given the preeminence in all homes.

The corporate witness of a body of believers, the local church, attuned to God in the spirit of worship, makes manifest a work of God, and gives credibility to the preaching of the Gospel, a teaching ministry. Every member is an extension of an arm of the local church that reaches out to the community wherein one lives, and to regions beyond. Some will start new churches, subsidized by the parent church. One's daily life and walk with Jesus exemplify the impact the ministry of the church is having on one's own life. It is an invitation to others to come and have a part in the worship of God.

In a church wherein diversities of gifts by the Holy Spirit are exercised to the edification of all, hearts will be enlarged for God and for each other, and new births experienced. When nurtured by the Word of God, there will be spiritual growth. "As newborn babes, desire the sincere milk of the word, that ye may grow thereby: If so be ye have tasted that the Lord is gracious" (1 Pet. 2:2-3).

All who are identified with the local church may not have yet come to experience the new birth. "So then Faith cometh by hearing, and hearing by the word of God" (Rom. 10:17). One cannot be saved from a spiritual kind of death, as one relates to God, unto a spiritual kind of life by an exercise of the will alone. It is the response of the whole man (the intellect, the emotions, the will, and the conscience) to the lover of one's soul. One who talks another into accepting Jesus as one's personal Savior is not only infracting the work of the Holy Spirit, but will probably get a response that is self-serving, and can possibly give one a false hope. "Jesus answered and said unto them, This is the work of God, that ye believe on him whom he hath sent" (John 6:29).

Man instinctively has a consciousness of being incomplete apart from a personal bond to God, and apart from family bonds, the home, and the church. What one hears of God at home will likely be what one hears of God at church. It is hoped that a teaching ministry unveils the historical revelation God has given of Himself that culminates in Jesus Christ.

Knowledge of God is not innate, so how can one come to know God? Tokens of God's love are in the world of nature all about us. While they are impersonal in character, they carry a personal message. The revelation of God made manifest in Jesus Christ is personal in character. "No man hath seen God at any time; the only begotten Son, which is in the bosom of the Father, he hath declared him" (John 1:18). "Philip saith unto him, 'Lord, shew us the Father, and it sufficeth us.' Jesus saith unto him, 'Have I been so long time with you, and yet hast thou not known me, Philip? he that hath seen me hath seen the Father; and how sayest thou then, Shew us the Father?'" (John 14:8-9). Jesus is the image of the Father, a personal revelation of God in human terms, a media with which all can relate.

What is taught in making Jesus known is all inclusive in the Gospel message. What one learns of Jesus is made effectual in one's heart by the quickening power of the Holy Spirit. Faith in Jesus can be no greater than the revelation one has of Jesus. A consciousness of Jesus' love for one is no less a consciousness of God's love for one, and, when it becomes revelation, will instinctively enkindle a responsive love for God. Love begets love. It is a spiritual phenomenon unexplainable, but known to the believer. The Apostle Paul said to the Corinthians, "Examine your own selves, whether ye be in the faith; prove your own selves" (II Cor. 13:5).

The home and the church are spiritual entities, and family-oriented. The home, wherein God is given preeminence, will have the abiding presence of God. The children will first learn of God's love for them from their parents, and again from the ministry of the church. The home propagates the race and the culture, and is the basic unit of the church. When God is not given the preeminence in the home, and respect for family values is lost, the church will also suffer. The response to the church's message propounding faith in Jesus is most apt to be self-serving, lacking love for God. When the home and the church fail in their respective stewardships to God, man's moorage will have been loosened by strong undercurrents, situation ethics, and the like, and all of society will suffer.

The third domain of God's Righteous Order is the State. It will be considered very briefly. It subjects man to law and order as one is related to others in civil, political, and industrial life. Unlike the Home and the Church, the State is a legal entity. The State determines civil rights, registers deeds and liens, and provides fire and police protection, schools, social welfare, and other legalities of all kinds.

The Apostle Paul admonishes Christians to live peaceably among all people as much as possible. (Rom. 12:18) In a democracy, one is to keep informed on political issues, and to exercise voting privileges for the sake of righteousness. The believer is the salt of the earth. (Matt. 5:13) He is a preservative of righteousness as he fits into society, being an example of good and a buffer against evil.

God gives the State authority to foster righteousness, to war against evil, to punish the lawless, and to keep a peaceable society. It is the will of God that man subject himself to this authority. The Apostle Paul asserted his Roman citizenship (Acts 22:27). The chief captain honored him as a citizen of the State. God is honored when man is subject to all authority vested by Him.

God's Recompensing Judgments
Part IV

The recompensing judgments of God are spiritual in character, consequential, not penal. They differ from all other judgments of God in that they address the inner man, the kind of person one is, one's spiritual stature. Only God knows the response one gives to His love, and one's faithfulness in stewardship. One is unmindful of what is happening to oneself by the personal choices one is making: the consequences of the degree to which one's heart is given to God. In time, one is unwittingly and consequentially determining one's own spiritual stature to be lived out in eternity: also one's celestial glory. What could be more sobering than to ponder the subject of God's recompensing judgments?

"By faith Moses, when he was come to years, refused to be called the son of Pharaoh's daughter; choosing rather to suffer affliction with the people of God, than to enjoy the pleasures of sin for a season; esteeming the reproach of Christ greater riches than the treasures in Egypt: for he had respect unto the recompense of the reward" (Heb. 11:24-26). When one is taught redemption from a legal premise the recompensing judgments of God are not likely to be addressed by the proponents of this theory. It is probably true that most people give no thought to God's recompensing judgments, or to living with the consequences of one's choices, good or evil. Forgiveness does not negate the consequences of sin. Sin debases one's spiritual stature: it affects the kind of person one is becoming.

Jesus said, "A good man out of the good treasure of his heart bringeth forth that which is good; and an evil man out of the evil treasure of his heart bringeth forth that which is evil: for of the abundance of the heart his mouth speaketh" (Luke 6:45). One's personal stature didn't just happen, but is consequential to the personal choices one makes from early youth.

It is innate in man to have a consciousness of God's love, and of being incomplete apart from God. It is as natural for a child to have a responsive interest in learning of God's love, as it is for a baby to instinctively root to feed from its mother's breast. "As newborn babes, desire the sincere milk of the word, that ye may grow thereby: if so be ye have tasted that the Lord is gracious" (1 Pet. 2:2-3).

Man's only relationship to God is spiritual or personal in character. God is Spirit, is essentially personality, life, and love. God makes manifest Himself, wherein one can personally interact with God's love, as a child responds to the caring caresses of a mother's love. Natural creation carries a message of God's love a child can receive; it readily reveals a communique from God. It isn't likely that a child can personally relate to God's love when taught from a legal premise: that Jesus died on the cross to pay one's debt of sin; that all who accept Jesus Christ as one's personal Savior will go to heaven. A child's mind can be programmed to think from a legal premise, but one's thoughts of God are apt to be more academic than revelation. A child may accept Jesus as his personal Savior, and rest on that decision, without having had any personal interaction with Jesus. Try to share with this child, some years later, thoughts of God's redeeming love from a spiritual or faith premise. His response is likely to be that he is saved, has accepted Jesus Christ as his Savior. A response, having been made from a legal premise, is not likely open to be addressed again.

The gospel of God's redeeming love is essentially spiritual in essence, even when declared from a legal premise, otherwise the message it bears wouldn't reach the heart.

Responses exacted by legal means are without spiritual value, and may be hurtful, giving one a false hope.

Making a commitment of oneself to Jesus, or accepting Jesus Christ as one's personal Savior, may or may not be saving faith, but is a step in the right direction. The subtlety of it is that the exercise of faith in Jesus can be objectively impersonal, not motivated by love for God; it can be self-serving.

Faith in, and love for Jesus are personal choices that have spiritual value only when they express one's heart. It isn't possible to tell another how to fall in love with Jesus or how to be saved.

The faculty of faith is a gift from God. The exercise of faith is personal. One's faith in Jesus can be objectively personal or objectively impersonal. All choices can be either positive or negative. I am addressing them separately in one's faith in Jesus.

One's faith in Jesus that is motivated by love for God is positive, is objectively personal. There is a personal interaction with Jesus that makes one become more like Jesus in character. It is like the qualities of character admired in another that unconsciously is adopted in one's own life. The greater faith one has in Jesus, the more Jesus is endeared to one's heart. This amounts to a personal bonding of one's heart to Jesus, wherein one literally lays down one's life for Jesus. One partakes of the life of Jesus, the life given Jesus by the Father and imparted to all believers. One will have a consciousness of being complete in Him, of Jesus' constant presence, a life lived to God's glory and man's fulfillment.

One's faith in Jesus that is not motivated by love for God is negative; is objectively impersonal; is in some way self-serving. It is like having faith in Jesus for what He can do for one: answer prayer, heal the sick, bring circumstances to pass that are favorable, and the like. There is no personal interaction with Jesus.

When one's concepts of God are built on a legal premise, patterned after Israel's covenant identity with God, one's relationship to God will be impersonal. When one does what is required: observing the ordinances of baptism and the Lord's Supper, and walking uprightly the best one can, one concludes one is acceptable to God. From a legal premise, there is no personal involvement with Jesus, no living bond to God as man was created to have.

Our Lord said, "No man cometh unto the Father but by me" (John 14:6). Man's only access to the Father is in identity with Jesus Christ. Only by faith in Jesus, faith motivated by love for God, is life mediated from the Father to the believer.

Motivation determines the spiritual value of the choices one makes. Choices not motivated by love are in some way self-serving. The subtlety of it is that one is not consciously mindful of the spiritual value of the choices one makes. They emanate from the inner man spontaneously, and unwittingly declare one's heart.

The responses of faith and love grow as one learns of Jesus, and the love of God made manifest. It is a growing endearment to God, experienced as if in a romance. The Holy Spirit takes the things of God and makes them revelation to one. The magnetic power of God's love draws a responsive heart to literally lay down one's life for Jesus. "This is the work of God, that ye believe on him whom he hath sent" (John 6:29). Time is the essence: saving faith is climactic to one's faith in Jesus motivated by love for God, as one's marriage is to a romance.

Faith in Jesus can be no greater than one's knowledge of Jesus, and one's love for God can be no greater than the love of God made manifest.

The declaring of the Gospel is a teaching ministry. The full disclosure of what is written on the subject of redemption allows for a progressive unveiling of the historical revelation God is giving of Himself that culminated in Jesus

Christ. A teaching ministry is enlightening to all ages of spiritual maturity. Saving faith is all-inclusive of falling in love with the lover of one's soul. It is a response of the whole man: the will, the intellect, the emotions, and the conscience, all-inclusive. Those who are saved from a spiritual kind of death know that Jesus is resident in their hearts. Jesus will be as much of an integral part of one's life as a devoted husband and wife are in each other. The love of God constrains one to walk uprightly. The spontaneity of one's actions to be found pleasing to God is an indication of how much one's heart is in it.

The spiritual relationship one has with God is consequential to the sum of one's choices made in a lifetime. This subject has been addressed at length, simply because it is the criterion, the basis of God's judgment, that determines man's spiritual stature in time, the saved and the lost. There will be degrees of celestial glory and of damnation in eternity.

God will render to every person a just recompense. "How shall we escape if we neglect so great salvation?" (Heb. 2:3) The judgment one hears will be voiced by the man Christ Jesus in His glorified manhood. "Because he hath appointed a day, in the which he will judge the world in righteousness by that man whom he hath ordained; whereof he hath given assurance unto all men, in that he hath raised him from the dead" (Acts 17:31). "For as the Father hath life in himself; so hath he given to the Son to have life in himself; and hath given him authority to execute judgment also, because he is the Son of man. Marvel not at this: for the hour is coming, in the which all that are in the graves shall hear his voice, and shall come forth, they that have done good, unto the resurrection of life; and they that have done evil, unto the resurrection of damnation. I can of mine own self do nothing: as I hear, I judge: and my judgment is just; because I seek not mine own will, but the will of the Father which hath sent me" (John 5:26-30).

The Son of God in His Divine nature is essentially life, an attribute He will always have by eternal generation. When He assumed manhood, He self-limited His Divine nature to the confines of human nature, making Himself subject to and dependent on the Father as is all of manhood. The life the Father gave the Son is to the manhood He assumed: to have life in Himself. He is man in a living bond to the Father as God created man to be. He is titled the Son of Man, having identified Himself with man. He is the only man with Divine heritage. He has authority delegated from the Father to execute judgment over the sons of man. Who else could qualify to voice the judgments of God? Jesus had discernment, knew what was in man, but having limited His Divine nature to the confines of human nature could not exercise omniscience. The judgments He voiced were the words of the Father transmitted through the Son in His glorified manhood: life to those who have done good, and damnation to those who have done evil.

The rewards of celestial glory will be addressed when all believers appear before the judgment seat of Christ. "For we must all appear before the judgment seat of Christ; that every one may receive the things done in his body, according to that he hath done, whether it be good or bad" (2 Cor. 5:10). Everyone will hear God's judgment on one's stewardship, an affirmation of one's faithfulness of a lifetime to God's glory: a determination only God can make, and again voiced by Jesus in His glorified manhood. The celestial glory that awaits one will be a place of distinction in the kingdom of God to be lived to God's glory throughout eternity.

There are judgments of God that do not address the inner man; are not relevant to the personal choices one makes in the kind of person one is becoming.

The judgments of God under the terms of the Old Covenant are a good example. God promised Israel blessings for keeping covenant and curses for breaking covenant.

The judgments fell upon Israel collectively: the innocent and guilty alike. The prevailing spirit determined the kind of judgment. Unlike the recompensing judgments, they were impersonal in character and temporal in duration.

There are providential judgments of God visited upon people collectively where the spirit of wickedness prevails. They are a lasting warning to all peoples who profane the righteousness of God. The judgments of the Great Flood, of Babel, and of Sodom and Gomorrah are examples. However, when warnings of impending judgments are heeded, they are stayed by God, as when Nineveh repented upon hearing the preaching of Jonah in Chapter 3 of the Book of Jonah. The message the judgments of God carry is a mercy of God and a warning to man. Those who get the message heed the warning; the hearts of those who do not are hardened. One can literally sin away his day of grace.

There is always a voice for God in the land. Upon hearing the preaching of Noah, no doubt many repented of their sin and believed God. When the flood waters came, those who repented were also drowned, but awakened to be in Paradise.

The Apostle Paul, in his epistle to the Romans, addressed the judgment of God on impenitent hearts in context with the subject on sodomy: God gave them up unto vile affections; God gave them over to reprobate minds (Rom. 1:24-32).

In my opinion, it is reasonable to relate the epidemic of the AIDS virus to a providential judgment of God. It is becoming worldwide, infecting the sexually inordinate and the innocent by contagion. There are no evidences of the gays repenting or turning from their lifestyle; they seem to be getting bolder in their shame, even wanting recognition as an entity in our society and a voice in church and government. Every effort is being given by medical research to find a treatment for the disease. The government is actively involved through the Department of Education and Health, mainly in preventive measures, some of which condone or license sin; some are burdensome to standard procedures proven to be effectually safe over the years. Every possibility of contagion is being addressed apart from moral implications. Lifestyles are not addressed. Spiritual values or guidelines are not even a consideration. If the AIDS virus is a providential judgment of God, man has not gotten the message.

When God is not given the preeminence by ordained authority vested by Him, and God's Standard of Righteousness is no longer the ruling ethic of man's behavior, self-interests will prevail. Most critical to our nation is the spiritual status of the home. The home is the basic unit of society. When God is not revered in the home, family values will have been lost. All of society suffers. It could be that a providential judgment of God is coming to our nation. President Calvin Coolidge, over seventy years ago, said, "The home is the citadel of American freedom, when the home is gone, America is gone."

Appendix A

In reading my book, there will no doubt be questions raised that ought to be addressed by the author. The first subject will be on the verity of the lapse of Adam. I want my reader to bear with me while I explain the relationship Adam and Eve had with God.

God created Adam and Eve in His own image. They were created personalities, could exercise free agency, make choices, were created flawless, were in a state of innocence but peccable—were vulnerable to temptation. In their flawless state, all of their thoughts would have been in keeping with the character of God. The choices they made would have been motivated by love for God. God was sharing His life with Adam and Eve in a relationship singular to them.

Adam and Eve lived in a paradise of God's making. They were in harmony with the world of nature, in communion with God in the spirit of worship, and with each other in the spirit of devotion. They had the joy of an ever present consciousness of God's love for them. The depraved man cannot relate to this kind of utopia, nor with Adam and Eve in their flawless state. Thus he wrongly accuses Eve of thoughts and actions that are self-serving, and Adam of unbelief. The only way that Adam or Eve could have been tempted to sin would have been in circumstances in which they were unaware of inordinate behavior.

The world of nature was Adam's domain in which he shared his life with Eve. The warmth of God's love for them would have given them unguarded security. The freedom they enjoyed was a consequence of being as God created them to be: bearing His image and sharing His life.

Being complete in each other follows being complete in God.

Adam and Eve were subject to temptation from without their flawless state, not from within; fallen man is subject to temptation from within and from without his flawed state.

Adam was no doubt subject to direction from God, as a child is from its father. God spoke a positive precept to Adam, pre-warning him of the consequences of disobedience. Adam shared the word of God with Eve. Both of them understood the precept, but in no way could either have related to the consequences of disobedience.

God made man a little lower than the angels; crowned him with glory and honor; set him over the works of His hands. There is nothing more rewarding to man than being given to God in faithful stewardship. Adam and Eve were fully occupied and wholly unaware of the possibility of an intrusion by an avenging spirit. They were literally open prey for an unexpected predator. Eve was no match for Satan, who, being powerless to strike at God, avenged his enmity by striking at the image of God. Eve's encounter with Satan was addressed in the early chapters of this treatise.

The Scriptures simply say that Eve was deceived, that Adam was not deceived (1 Tim. 2:14) and by the disobedience of one man many were made sinners (Rom. 5:17-19). Adam was disobedient. There is no place in the Scriptures where Adam or Eve is associated with unbelief. Disobedience and unbelief are both sins, but are not synonymous: cannot be used interchangeably.

Disobedience is failing to obey. Unbelief is counter to or the opposite of faith. Adam, in his flawless state, could not have been charged with unbelief. The depraved man is not flawless, so can be guilty of unbelief. This would include all of fallen manhood. Disobedience does not necessarily imply unbelief. It can be inadvertent with no intent of a personal offense against God. However, the disobedient are guilty of sin and will suffer the personal consequences of sin.

Eve, deceived by the subtlety of Satan's words, "took of the fruit thereof, and did eat, and gave also unto her husband with her, and he did eat" (Gen. 3:6). This is of record in one sentence, Gen. 3:6, and is the only direct account of the fall of man in the Scriptures. There is no room between the lines for one to build a doctrine by conjecture. There was nothing inordinate in Adam taking food given unto him by his wife and eating it. Upon eating thereof together, their eyes were opened to the consequence of their sin. They were lost to a living bond to God.

The only logical and reasonable conclusion is that Adam's disobedience was made while he was momentarily in a lapse. In a lapse, one's mind is disengaged from what he is doing; one's actions are without motivation. Motivation is a determining factor in one's intent. There are no grounds to charge Adam with personal intent in his disobedience to God. He suffered the personal consequence and guilt incurred by his disobedience, but not a penal judgment.

Appendix B

The second subject to be addressed is in answer to the question: How could Adam and Eve have been flawless yet vulnerable to temptation?

Adam and Eve were created in the image of God, flawless. Man in his fallen state cannot relate to Adam and Eve in their flawless state. The subject can only be addressed from what is written. When God looked upon what He had created, He saw that it was good, very good. God cannot be adjudged guilty of having created that which was with flaw.

The latitude God gave man to express free agency is inclusive of man having been a created personality. To say that man is peccable or vulnerable to temptation is synonymous with saying human nature has latitude to express free agency. Our Lord is impeccable: His Divine nature is self-limited to the confines of the human nature He assumed: being Divine by eternal generation, He cannot sin.

Allowing the exercise of self-expression, Adam and Eve were vulnerable to temptation, not from within their flawless state, but to that which was from without. Eve was no match for the wiles of Satan. Eve was deceived. "She took of the fruit thereof, and did eat, and gave also to her husband with her; and he did eat." Adam was not deceived. What Adam did in his flawless state couldn't have been an act of sin against God or self-serving. The taking of the fruit given him by Eve and eating thereof must have been without thought, a lapse in what he was doing, but no less disobedience. Both Adam and Eve sinned and suffered a spiritual kind of death and a depraved nature as they related to God. Consequently all of Adam's posterity are born flawed; all are born vulnerable to temptation from within and from without one's flawed state. It is no wonder one cannot relate to Adam and Eve in their flawless state.

A glass vase can be perfect crystal, and flawless. By the very nature of glassware, however, it is vulnerable to breakage, but the break will come from without the vase, not from within.

Appendix C

All theories have suppositions for the truth that are subject to being supplanted when proven false. The vicarious theory of the atonement is no exception. There have been a number of theories on the atonement, the vicarious theory being one. It is taught as a fact, but is a theory, and is subject to the same scrutiny as are all theories.

I have said that spiritual values are not made effectual in one's heart by legal means. This is not altogether true. The Ten Commandments are essentially spiritual. They are no less spiritual in context with the terms of the Old Covenant which is legal in character. God's love got through to the hearts of innumerable Israelites to effect a responsive love for God. Millions of Christians have professed faith in Jesus Christ upon hearing the Gospel presented from a legal premise. This in itself does not prove the theory to be the whole truth. My ministry had been from the same premise prior to heeding personal convictions to re-examine the subject. It had bothered me that the response of faith in Jesus upon hearing the Gospel presented from a legal premise was not necessarily saving faith. One's response can be self-serving. Only faith in Jesus motivated by love for God is saving faith. Motivation determines the spiritual value of all personal actions. The Apostle Paul rejoiced in that Christ is preached, whether in pretense or in truth (Phil. 1:18).

The Gospel message is that God is reconciled to man: the bid of the Gospel is for man to be reconciled to God through faith in Jesus Christ. Jesus is come to deliver man from a spiritual kind of death as one relates to God unto a spiritual kind of life. The declaring of the Gospel is a teaching ministry and must be taught in ways with which one can personally relate to God.

The Gospel presented from a spiritual premise addresses the inner man: invites a personal interaction with the lover of one's soul: a dying to oneself to be in a living bond to Jesus. It is like the spiritual bonding of two hearts, made effectual in a romance, and culminated in a marriage. It is this kind of bonding that endears God to one, and a husband and wife to each other. God's objective in the creation and redemption of man is that He might share His life with man.

It is innate in man to be consciously incomplete apart from God, as the boy and girl, upon reaching puberty, are to each other. To be complete in God and in each other comes naturally and does not need to be primed by inductive means. There is no way one can tell another how to fall in love.

As one relates to God, it is the hearing of God's love in ways with which one can relate that effects a responsive love to God's love for one: a magnetic phenomenon that is unexplainable. We love Him because He first loved us. Love begets love. Love is the laying down of one's life for another.

There is no way a child can personally relate to Jesus dying on the cross in payment of a debt incurred by one's sin. Death to satisfy a penal judgment for one's sin is not relevant to a child's thinking. One's relationship to God is spiritual in character, not legal. A child can sense the caring attention given it by another. It is unexplainable. The mother's love in faithfully caring for her child begets a responsive love for the mother. The mother has an aura of love about her that her child can sense. The child will want to be found pleasing to its mother. This same spiritual phenomenon is true as a child learns of God's caring love. Spiritual growth is consequential to the personal responses one gives to the revelation God is giving of Himself.

It doesn't sound reasonable to address the innocent in terms of guilt as they relate to God. All are born in a depraved state; are prone to sin and given to that which is self-serving, but not one is born in a state of unbelief. All sins shall be forgiven unto the sons of men, save for the sin of unbelief. It is unbelief that condemns one. Only God knows when one's heart reaches the state of unbelief.

The above quote precludes any thought of equating salvation with forgiveness. One who is responsive to God's forgiveness is restored to the relationship to God before the offense, but it doesn't make one's sin as though it never happened. Sin causes one to suffer a personal loss, affecting one's spiritual stature, the kind of person one is becoming, but not a penal judgment. One's responsibility and accountability cannot be assumed by another vicariously. The personal choices one makes in time as one relates to God will be the determining factor of one's celestial glory in eternity and of one's state of condemnation when not included in the family of God.

That Christ died for our sins is not to be found in the Four Gospels, or in the Acts of the Apostles, but is found in other books of the New Testament.

Dean Alford, an authority in translating Greek to English, comments on 1 Cor. 15:3, Christ died for our sins according to the scriptures. He states that the word "for," in the context, should read "on behalf of" our sins: an atonement for our sins. Atonement is spiritual in character and offered in the sanctuary of worship, and not by the order of a court of law.

"Christ died on the cross for our sins" is not to be found anywhere in the Bible. "On the cross" is not a translation, but a supposition inserted long ago in the phrase "Christ died for our sins" by the proponents of the vicarious theory of the atonement. It makes our Lord's death satisfy a penal judgment of death on sin in the sinner's stead vicariously. To hold Christ's death on the cross as payment of a penal judgment would be a legal transaction by works not by faith.

The payment of a penal judgment of death on sin is not relevant to the spiritual kind of death man is suffering as he relates to God. It isn't one's sin that keeps one from a living bond to God, but unbelief.

The personal sacrifices made by the Father and the Son to redeem fallen man are spiritual in character. Redemption is expressive of God's love for man to the uttermost. What is in the heart of God in eternity is made manifest to man in time. There is no time factor with God in eternity.

The personalities of the Father and the Son are exclusive of each other, but have attributes in common and are in full accord. They acted simultaneously in redeeming fallen man, each respectively sacrificing that which endeared them the most to each other.

The Father gave His Son never to have Him back again on the Divine level, but on the human level. The Son gave of Himself, self-limiting His Divine nature to the confines of human nature. He made Himself subject to the Father as are all of mankind.

To my knowledge the spiritual manhood the Son of God assumed in eternity has not been addressed heretofore. It was in His spiritual manhood the Father appointed His Son to be the Great High Priest over all of fallen man: a distinction of honor bestowed only by God (Heb. 5:1-6). "Who verily was foreordained before the foundation of the world, but was manifest in these last times for you" (1 Pet. 1:20). The first rite He officiated was in the offering of Himself in identity with and on the behalf of fallen man to atone for the sins of the whole world, an offering acceptable to the Father. All sins will be forgiven the sons of men, save for the sin of unbelief.

In eternity, before the world was, God is reconciled to man. The Gospel beseeches man to be reconciled to God through faith in Jesus Christ, faith motivated by love for

God. Faith in Jesus can be no greater than one's knowledge of Jesus, and one's love for God no greater than God's love made manifest. Faith and love are made known to the uttermost from what is of holy writ on the subject of redemption.

God's objective in redemption is the restoration of the life with God that man lost in the fall. The kind of death man suffered and the life recovered are spiritual in character. The Son in assuming human nature becomes the channel of life from the Father to all who will be identified with the family of God through faith in Jesus Christ. God sent His Son into the world on a spiritual mission to redeem man from a spiritual kind of death, unto a spiritual kind of life, as one relates to God.

The rituals of worship ordained by God carried the message of redemption to all peoples until all that was prefigured of Jesus in type was fulfilled in His person at His coming. The promises of God and the cherished hopes of all believers rested in Him. He was made like unto His brethren, sin apart. He was revelation of the living bond to the Father man was created to have. He came to seek out His bride, inclusive of all believers, collectively, and by adoption, members of the family of God, citizens of the Kingdom of Heaven, an expansion of the Divine family. All believers faithfully worship the Father in family bonds as their Father and their God.

The Son was sent by the Father into the world in His spiritual manhood, to assume His mortal body prepared for Him in the womb of the virgin Mary: "A body thou has prepared me." The prenatal fetus in the womb of the virgin Mary had biological life, but not spiritual life. When Mary gave birth, our Lord assumed the body of His mortal manhood. He was revelation of a relationship to the Father that all of manhood was created to have.

Jesus was made like unto His brethren, sin apart. Mortal manhood is all inclusive of a life cycle, a time to be born and a time to die. He could not have assumed for another that which was single to Him alone. In assuming mortal manhood, He had but one life cycle. It was terminated when His mortal body put on immortality. Proponents of the vicarious theory say that He could die for the sins of all of manhood and live, because He is God. The reasoning is neither logical nor the truth, because He was God self-limited to the confines of the mortal manhood He assumed. His relationship to man was spiritual in character, not legal.

The rituals of worship ordained by God prefigured in type what would be fulfilled in Jesus Christ at His coming. They were to be observed by all peoples. The worship of God is spiritual in character, not legal. To build a theory of redemption on a legal premise is a departure from worship ordained by God.

The Father's love motivated Him to say: "Let us make man in our image and after our likeness." It was the objective of the divine family to enlarge the family of God by the adoption of sons, all believers . . . "In eternity the delights of the Father and the Son were in the sons of men . . . " (paraphrased from Prov. 8:23-31).

Appendix D

God the Father and His only begotten Son are spirits, are personalities. The sacrifices they made of themselves in redeeming fallen man are spiritual in character. The personalities of the Son and the Father are exclusive of each other. For example: the personality of my son is exclusive of my personality. The actions and responses of one are independent of the other. One may have a greater appreciation of the sacrifices of love made by the Father and the Son in redeeming fallen man, knowing that they are two personalities acting independently, simultaneously, and spontaneously in full accord.

The Father gave His only begotten Son never to have Him back again on the Divine level. The Son gave of Himself in self-limiting His Divine nature to the confines of human nature. He assumed His spiritual manhood in eternity before time. There is no flesh and blood in eternity. "Flesh and blood cannot inherit the kingdom of God" (1 Cor. 15:50). I may be introducing a subject that has not crossed the minds of my readers heretofore: to think of the spiritual manhood the Son of God assumed in eternity, apart from His body.

God created man bipartite, body and spirit. "And the Lord God formed man of the dust of the ground, and breathed into his nostrils the breath of life; and man became a living soul" (Gen. 2:7). The spirit is the personality; the body houses the spiritual man.

The Son in assuming His spiritual manhood made His relationship to the Father on the human level. God the Father becomes His Father and His God.

"Jesus saith unto her, 'Mary.' She turned herself, and saith unto him, 'Rabboni:' which is to say, 'Master.' Jesus saith unto her, 'Touch me not; for I am not yet ascended to my Father: but go to my brethren, and say unto them, I ascend unto my Father, and your Father; and to my God, and your God'" (John 20:16-17). Also, in assuming manhood, He made Himself subject to the Father as is all of manhood.

Many verses of Scripture throw light upon that which is before time. For example, from John 17:5 we learn of the glorious relationship the Son was having with the Father in His spiritual manhood before time: "And now, O Father, glorify thou me with thine own self with the glory which I had with thee before the world was" (John 17:5).

The message of Heb. 5:5 and Ps. 2:7 is also a good example. "Thou art my Son, this day have I begotten thee" is not a calendar date, but the eternal state of the only begotten Son of God. In the context of Heb. 5:4-6, the Father calls His only begotten Son to be the Great High Priest over all of fallen manhood, an honor bestowed only by God. He assumed His priestly office in His spiritual manhood, and officiated the first rite of worship in the offering of Himself on behalf of and in identity with fallen man, to atone for the sins of the whole world.

The Son of God in His spiritual manhood is without His mortal body. He is also incomplete apart from His bride, as Adam was without Eve. God sent His Son into the world in His spiritual manhood to assume the body the Father prepared for Him in the womb of the virgin Mary, and to gather together His bride, all believers.

The scriptures, many times, throw enough light on a subject to allow for reasonable conjecture. All that is reasonable and logical may or may not be the truth, but all that is of the truth will be reasonable and logical. The writer associates the words of our Lord, "a body hast thou prepared me" (Heb. 10:5), with that Holy thing in the womb of the virgin Mary. "And the angel said unto her, 'Fear not, Mary: for thou hast found favour with God. And, behold, thou shalt conceive in thy womb, and bring forth a son, and shalt call his name JESUS' . . . Then said Mary unto the angel, 'How shall this be, seeing I know not a man?' And the angel answered and said unto her, 'The Holy Ghost shall come upon thee and the power of the Highest shall overshadow thee: therefore also that Holy thing which shall be born of thee shall be called the Son of God'" (Luke 1:30-31, 34-35).

Mary's conception was not by natural generation, but the body was of God's forming—biological life apart from spiritual life: miraculous indeed, but no more so than God forming the body of man from the dust of the ground. "For with God nothing shall be impossible" (Luke 1:37). She carried that Holy thing in her womb the full term of her pregnancy. At birth, simultaneous with the biological body taking its first breath, the Son of God in His spiritual manhood took residency in the body prepared for Him by the Father. Upon assuming His mortal body, He is the whole man, body and spirit. It was the life cycle of the mortal body he assumed—offered once, a living sacrifice to the Father. The lamb slain from the foundation of the world has no termination: the Son of God is offering Himself in His glorified manhood in eternity.

He was made like unto His brethren, sin apart. He is the only perfect man, as He is Divine by eternal generation: the only man with Divine heritage. He is revelation to fallen man of the living bond to the Father man was created to have, a relationship that is not mockery, but one of hope, made personal in one's response to God's redeeming love: faith in Jesus motivated by love for God.

Agent for Dr. Paul A. Dewhirst
JPA Associates
P.O. Box 20226
El Cajon, CA 92021